Othello In Wonderland
and
Mirror-Polishing
Storytellers

Bibliotheca Iranica
Performing Arts Series

[*Unnumbered*]
M.R. Ghanoonparvar and John Green
Iranian Drama: An Anthology
(0-939214-63-3; 1989)

Number 1
Parviz Sayyad
Theater of Diaspora
(0-939214-94-6; 1993)

Number 3 (forthcoming)
Dariush Tala'i
Traditional Persian Art Music
The *Radif* of Mirza Abdullah
(1-56859-039-9; 1997)

Bibliotheca Iranica
Performing Arts Series
Number 2

Othello In Wonderland
and
Mirror-Polishing Storytellers

Two Plays By

Gholamhoseyn Sa`edi

Edited, With An Introduction And Notes, By
M. R. Ghanoonparvar

Translated From The Persian By
Michael Phillips With M. R. Ghanoonparvar

Critical Essay By
Kaveh Safa

Mazda Publishers
Costa Mesa, California
1996

Mazda Publishers
Since 1980
P.O. Box 2603
Costa Mesa, California 92626 U.S.A.
Homepage: http://www.mazdapub.com

Library of Congress Cataloging-in-Publication Data

Sā`idī, Ghulām Ḥusayn.
[Utillū dar sarzamīn-i `ajāyib. English]
Othello in Wonderland; and Mirror-polishing Storytellers/ two plays
by Gholamhoseyn Saedi; edited, with an introduction and notes by
M.R. Ghanoonparvar; translation from the Persian by Michael
Phillips; critical essay by Kaveh Safa.
p.cm.—(Bibliotheca Iranica: Performing Arts Series, No. 2)
Includes bibliographical references.

ISBN:1-56859-046-6
(pbk.:alk. paper)

1. Censorship—Iran—Drama. 2. Iran—Social conditions—1979—
Drama. 3. Sā`idī, Ghulām Ḥusayn—Criticism and interpretation.
I. Ghanoonparvar, M.R. (Mohammad R.) II. Phillips, Michael, d.
1992. III. Safa, Kaveh. IV. Sā`idī, Ghulām Ḥusayn. Pardahdārān-i
ā'inah afrūz. English. V. Title. VI. Title: Mirror-polishing storytellers.
PK6561.S2706713 1996
891'.5523—dc21
96-44025
CIP

This volume is dedicated to the memory of
Gholamhoseyn Sa`edi
and
Michael Phillips

CONTENTS

Introduction

When in 1985 Gholamhoseyn Sa'edi (b. 1935) died in Paris, Iran lost not only its best known playwright, but also one of its most prolific writers of fiction, movie scripts, and essays. Sa'edi, who wrote his plays under the pen name Gowhar Morad, was a psychiatrist by profession. Despite his success as a psychiatrist, particularly his practice, which was often free of charge for the indigent in south Tehran, he was mainly known as an anti-establishment writer of the 1960s and 1970s, during the Pahlavi era, and again in the 1980s, after the Islamic Revolution, when he lived in exile in France.

The two plays presented in this volume in translation are among the last plays Sa'edi wrote in exile. In fact, these two plays were published posthumously in 1986, shortly after his death on November 24, 1985. Prior to his death, *Otello dar Sarzamin-e Ajayeb* [Othello in Wonderland] was staged in Persian, first in Paris and later in London. A videotape of the London production has been available in Europe and the United States, which may eventually prove to make *Othello in Wonderland* his most watched play. Efforts were also under way just prior to Sa'edi's death to stage a rather elaborate production of *Pardehdaran-e A'inehafruz* [Mirror-Polishing Storytellers], for which an Iranian artist, Bahram Amu-Oghli, had already prepared large canvas paintings.

Although this is the first volume devoted entirely to Sa'edi's plays, these are not his first works to be translated into English. Two other plays, for example, *Mah-e Asal* [Honeymoon] and *Karbafak-ha dar Sangar* [Workaholics in the Trenches] were included in *Iranian Drama: An Anthology* (compiled and edited by M. R. Ghanoonparvar and John Green; Costa Mesa, CA: Mazda Publishers, 1989). Also, several short stories by Sa'edi appear in various anthologies in translation as well as two collections of his short stories, *Dandil: Stories From Iranian Life* (translated by Robert

Campbell, Hasan Javadi, and Julie S. Meisami; New York: Random House, 1981) and *Fear and Trembling* (translated by Minoo Southgate; Washington, DC: Three Continents Press, 1984).

An important feature of Sa'edi's work in general is his focus on the socio-political issues of the day. His plays, short stories, ethnographic studies, film scripts, and other work in the 1960s and 1970s deal with the vital issues of those years, such as political oppression, censorship, social ills, poverty, and generally problems facing Iranians in a culture in transition from traditionalism to modernity. In his work in the 1980s as well, Sa'edi continued to address the important issues which faced his country. Each of the two plays in this volume, which were written since the Islamic Revolution in 1979 and the establishment of the Islamic Republic in Iran, deal with perhaps the two most immediate and vital issues of the first part of the 1980s in Iran, namely the effects of the new social order, with the new government threat against individual and artistic liberties, and the devastating effects of the longest military conflict in the twentieth century, the Iran-Iraq war.

Sa'edi had already written on the subject of censorship imposed by the new regime and voiced his opposition to the new Islamic social order in the form of essays and stories he published in *Alefba*, a literary journal he founded in Paris in the early 1980s. In *Othello in Wonderland*, he conducts a fictional case study of censorship and the clashes of views and ideologies between the officials and supporters of the Islamic regime and the secular intelligentsia of Iran. The play works on several levels and has something to offer to different audiences. To fully grasp Sa'edi's craftsmanship as a playwright and his thorough grasp of cultural conflicts in the play, one must be familiar with Shakespeare's *Othello* as well as the tradition of Shakespearean theater in Iran, but more importantly, for younger, secular Iranians, with the many nuances and intricacies of Shi'ite religious scholarship and traditional training in the seminaries in Qom and other centers in Iran, the graduates of which have now taken charge of the government and the daily life of that country. Sa'edi masterfully parodies the kind of "scholarly" debates that take place between the clerics from the seminaries and their like-minded counterparts in the universities. While the character of the Minister represents the Shi'ite clerics who attempt to catch up with the late twentieth-century world by pretending not only to understand but to be masters of every subject, even

Western art and technology, Professor Khorush and Professor Makhmalchi (both based on actual notables in post-revolutionary Iran) attempt to bridge the abyss that exists between modern scholarship and traditional or religious beliefs. Despite all its humor, the play is horrifying to many Iranian audiences who reside outside Iran, and also in Iran, particularly the secular writers, artists, and intellectuals. What is wrapped in the guise of humor rings to many as a true picture of the situation in which Iranians, in this case, those involved in the theater, face in their everyday working and living environment in Iran. While for the sake of humor Sa'edi indulges in exaggeration, at the same time, he achieves his desired effect on the audience in provoking their anti-regime sentiments. In this respect, the play functions as propaganda art and serves a political purpose as well.

In a similar vein, *Mirror-Polishing Storytellers* may be character-ized as propaganda art. In fact, its anti-war message is not merely implied but explicitly stated throughout the play and is particu-larly pronounced in the concluding scene, as the play ends with an anti-war chant, a sort of political rally. Despite overt political overtones, however, in *Mirror-Polishing Storytellers*, Sa'edi manipu-lates his audience with less direct but perhaps more effective devices to share his views. The gruesome scenes in which the parents of "martyred" soldiers fight over the body parts of the corpses, for instance, are devised to so disgust the audience or readers of the play that they can no longer concern themselves about ideologies or politics but react emotionally. Of course, the scenes in which various storytellers try to win the audience over to their point of view by reasoning are essentially overshadowed by the gruesome scenes in the cemetery and in fact help prepare the audience for the emotional episodes in the play.

An important aspect of *Mirror-Polishing Storytellers* is Sa'edi's use of the traditional *naqqal*s [storytellers], who were common in many cities and villages in Iran and who, aided by canvas paint-ings that depicted scenes from the Iranian national epic, the *Shahnameh* [The Book of Kings] by eleventh-century poet Ferdowsi or various battles and martyrdoms of Shi'ite holy figures, such as Imam Hoseyn, told stories to audiences that gathered around them in public squares, usually near cemeteries and shrines. These traveling storytellers would sometimes stretch a story for several hours, flavoring the main plot with all sorts of anecdotes and aphorisms, always appealing to the audience's emotions, thereby trying to extract a few coins from them. Sa'edi has masterfully tried to replicate the language and tone of these storytellers in his play. And for this reason, *Mirror-Polishing Storytellers*, like *Othello in Wonderland*, contains some very culture-specific language, a feature that presents the translator with a formidable challenge.

Several years ago, when Michael Phillips, who at the time was working on his doctoral dissertation at the University of Texas at Austin, suggested to me that he would like to translate these two plays (in addition to three Arabic plays) as a part of his thesis on translation theory and practice, even though I thought the plays were very important, I tried to dissuade him, given the difficulties inherent in these plays with regard to the rendition of the language as well as other cultural aspects of the plays. Michael Phillips, however, welcomed the challenge and began translating them. For more than a year, Michael met with me on a regular weekly basis to go over the portions he had translated. Having already participated in a joint translation project (a play, *Honeymoon*) some years earlier, he had developed his own philosophy and style in translation, of which I was quite aware. Michael had already asked me to write an introduction to the English translation of these two plays, which he planned to publish. Unfortunately, he was unable to complete the translations before his untimely death in 1992 . He had submitted an incomplete draft of a translation of *Othello in Wonderland* and about one-half of *Mirror-Polishing Storytellers*. It would have been Michael's wish to see these translations published.

In order to prepare these plays for publication, I have completed the missing portions of the first play and Scenes 1 through 6 of the second play. In editing the parts translated by Michael Phillips, I have tried to retain the essence and style of his translations, although certain changes have been made throughout the texts of both plays. I have also changed and systematized the transliteration system of Persian names and terms. The transliterations are based on Persian pronunciation. Diacritical marks have been avoided to make the reading less cumbersome. Traditional storytellers spice their stories with occasional verses. Sa'edi utilizes this tradition in *Mirror-Polishing Storytellers*, sometimes parodying famous classical or popular poems. To retain a flavoring of the original, I have rendered these lines as verse in English, hoping to recreate the sing-song effect the storytellers employ. In *Othello in Wonderland*, I have replaced Michael Phillips' English translations of Shakespeare's lines that appear in Persian in Sa'edi's play with the actual corresponding lines from Shakespeare's *Othello*.

The plays in this volume are followed by a critical essay by Kaveh Safa (first published in *Emergence* 2 [Spring 1990]) as well as an explanatory list of terms, names, and other items with which some English readers may not be familiar. Finally, I would like to thank John Bordie, who supported the idea of publishing Michael Phillips' translations, and Kaveh Safa, for agreeing to include his essay. I am also indebted to Hamid Naficy for his suggestion to include the Safa essay in this volume.

M. R. Ghanoonparvar
The University of Texas at Austin

Othello In Wonderland

Personae:

OTHELLO
DESDEMONA
IAGO
EMILIA
CASSIO
BIANCA
MINISTER OF ISLAMIC GUIDANCE
PROFESSOR KHORUSH
PROFESSOR MAKHMALCHI
REVOLUTIONARY GUARD
ZEYNAB SISTER
DIRECTOR
SECURITY OFFICER

The scene: The rehearsal studio of a theater, cluttered with knickknacks and junk. To one side is a large table on which are several ashtrays overflowing with butts, kleenexes, and a number of typed play scripts. There are several chairs here and there. A small bookcase. Several books and a small cassette recorder. One trunk here and there. A clothes rack with a few items of clothing. On the other side of the set is another table behind which several chairs have been arranged for spectators of the rehearsal. Between the two tables is the rehearsal area. In the center of the back wall is a little book case with a few disorganized books, and beside the bookcase is a large clothes rack with various costumes. On the other side of the bookcase is a mirror on the wall. Facing it is a table full of makeup supplies. Several chairs are scattered here and there. On one of the tables is a little recorder that is playing Iranian music. OTHELLO, IAGO, CASSIO and EMILIA are in the rehearsal area. DESDEMONA sits knitting a sweater to one side. IAGO paces while reading the script. Every few seconds he closes it and repeats under his breath the part he has memorized. OTHELLO sits on a chair and has his feet on a table. He is smoking a cigarette with his eyes closed. EMILIA is gathering the trash and throwing it into a wastebasket. She empties the ashtray in front of OTHELLO and puts it back in front of him. OTHELLO puts his cigarette out. CASSIO is stretched out on a bench.

OTHELLO: I'm tired of this. Let's forget it. We're never going to get anywhere.

IAGO: What? You're giving up?

OTHELLO: Giving up? I'd like to tear their hearts out. The creeps have kept us hanging on for five months now. They were supposed to give us permission for the play today.

DESDEMONA: Don't let it get to you.

CASSIO: To hell with them. If they don't give us permission, so what? We can put the play on somewhere or other ourselves.

IAGO: Sure. You think it's that simple?

CASSIO: Why not? If you want to do something, you just do it.

EMILIA: You sure are in a foul mood, man. [*She empties the ashtray in front of OTHELLO into the wastebasket and puts it back in front of him. OTHELLO puts out his cigarette in it.*] I hardly get it emptied before you dirty it up again.

OTHELLO: Are you forgetting that I'm your lord?

EMILIA: My lord?

OTHELLO: Have you forgotten Act Five, Scene Two?

EMILIA: What do you mean?

OTHELLO: You shout, "My lord, my lord, my lord!" You should read the play.

EMILIA: I've read it. I shout from offstage, "My lord, my lord!"

OTHELLO: Now, say it once on stage: "My lord!"

IAGO [*stops reading*]: What's with you two? I'm trying to work.

OTHELLO [*lights another cigarette*]: What do you mean, work?

IAGO: I'm memorizing a part I have to say to you, Othello, Your Excellency.

OTHELLO [*with a smirk*]: And which part would that be, Iago, sir?

IAGO [*acting, to OTHELLO*]: Stand you awhile apart,
Confine yourself but a patient list.
Whilst you were here o'erwhelmed with your grief
(A passion most unsuiting such a man),
Cassio came hither. I shifted him away...

OTHELLO [*indicates CASSIO*]: Look at that. Cassio's been sleeping like a log for an hour.

DESDEMONA: What's wrong with you? The poor guy's back hurts. He gets off work dead tired and needs to rest up.

OTHELLO [*laughs*]: You always take Cassio's side. Shakespeare must have made a mistake in the play. You two did have an affair, didn't you?

DESDEMONA [*puts the sweater on the floor and gets up and acts*]:
And have you mercy too! I never did
Offend you in my life; never lov'd Cassio...

OTHELLO [*gets up and acts*]: That handkerchief that I so lov'd, and gave thee,
Thou gav'st to Cassio.

IAGO [*throws his notebook on the table and applauds*]: Bravo, perfect.

CASSIO [*rolling over*]: Hey, guys, let me sleep for a minute.

OTHELLO: Shut up and drop dead! Two hours and the guy's still not back.

CASSIO: What guy?

OTHELLO: How many guys are there? His Highness, the director who has let us twiddle our thumbs for two hours.

DESDEMONA: He went to try to get a letter of permission, man. Didn't you know that?

IAGO [*looks at his watch*]: He left four hours ago. He should have been back by now.

CASSIO [*gets up from the cot*]: They only had to say yes or no. It couldn't have taken all this time.

EMILIA: Nowadays getting a letter of permission isn't such a piece of cake.

IAGO: What do you mean? He just went to consult with the authorities and obtain their consent.

CASSIO: Bianca isn't here either.

IAGO: Do you miss your beloved?

CASSIO: We should try calling. To hell with Bianca. Call the director, I mean.

IAGO: Where can we call him?

CASSIO: How do I know? At that hell-hole, what's its name? The Ministry of Islamic Guidance.

DESDEMONA: Shshshshsh, [*quietly*] somebody could be listening outside the door.

IAGO: We just called. And what did they say? [*In a rough voice*] There's no one by that name here, brother.

OTHELLO: I don't think he's going to get it.

IAGO: What a pessimist. We shouldn't be so pessimistic.

OTHELLO: You've really gotten into Iago. You always think that in the end you'll succeed at everything.

IAGO: But in the end I get killed by your hand. That's Iago's fate, isn't it?

OTHELLO: And what is my fate? I get killed, too.

IAGO: By whom?

OTHELLO [*angrily*]: By all of you. By this stinking, shitty world.

DESDEMONA: After you kill me, of course.

IAGO: Miss Desdemona, we're trying to have a serious discussion. [*To all the others*] In any case, I think since we are still just reading and we're not on the set yet, we should sit down and run over those bits that all four of us are in together.

EMILIA: I agree.

OTHELLO: Ok. Let's start.

IAGO: Good idea.

DESDEMONA: Be thou assured, good Cassio, I will do
All my abilities in thy behalf.

EMILIA: Good madam, do. I warrant it grieves my husband
As if the cause were his.

CASSIO: Bounteous madam,
Whatever shall become of Michael Cassio,
He's never anything but your true servant.

OTHELLO and IAGO in another corner.

IAGO: I do beseech you,
Though I perchance am vicious in my guess,
As I confess it is my nature's plague
To spy into abuses, and oft my jealousy
Shapes faults that are not,

OTHELLO: What dost thou mean?

IAGO: Good name in man and woman, dear my lord... [*Out of
character*] We know this already, let's skip down a little.

OTHELLO: Why, why is this?
Think'st thou I'd make a life of jealousy,
To follow still the changes of the moon
With fresh suspicions?

*All at once the door opens and the DIRECTOR enters happily with a
gunnysack in hand. He is very cheerful; puts the sack in a corner.*

DIRECTOR: Hey, guys! We're victorious! [*Takes a letter out of his
pocket and shows it to them.*]

OTHELLO: What are we?

DIRECTOR: I got it, I got it, I got it. [*Snaps his finger over his head
  and spins around with joy.*]

OTHELLO: Really? You got the permission?

IAGO: The permission letter?

DIRECTOR: I got it, I got it. You didn't think I would? [*The others
  applaud happily. In a loud voice*] Didn't I tell you I could
  fool them?

DESDEMONA: What's with you? [*Indicates the door with her hand.*]
  Someone might...

DIRECTOR [*catches himself. In a theatrical voice*]: This is a part of
  Scene Seven, in which... [*looks around with fear and trembling, while the others gather around.*] Yeah, guys, they really
  make it hard, but they're flaky and you can talk them into
  anything.

OTHELLO: Ok, read it; let's see.

DIRECTOR [*opens the envelope happily and takes out the letter. To
  EMILIA*]: Bring me a little water. [*Takes the glass of water
  from EMILIA, drinks it, and starts to read.*] "In the name of
  the Almighty. Permission is granted to the Damavand
  Troupe to stage the Elizabethan play Shakespeare by
  Othello."

OTHELLO: Huh, the play Shakespeare by Othello!

IAGO: Never mind, this kind of thing isn't their specialty.

DIRECTOR: They meant Othello by Shakespeare...

OTHELLO: But I... [*To IAGO*] That line where it says: First adorn
  it with the colors of the sky...

DIRECTOR: I'm sure it was just a typing error. Don't worry, I'll
  get it fixed.

DESDEMONA [to OTHELLO]: Forget it.

OTHELLO: Fine, fine.

DESDEMONA: Now, they've imposed several minor conditions, but they're not really important. [*The actors move away from the DIRECTOR, frowning.*]

CASSIO: Yeah, as it says in the play, "You advise me well."

DIRECTOR: Where?

CASSIO: Act Two, Scene Three.

DIRECTOR: Wait just a little, man, we're not rehearsing yet. [*Begins reading the rest of the permission letter.*] In producing the play, the conditions below must be met: "One, the use of obscene words is absolutely forbidden."

EMILIA: There aren't any obscene words in this play.

IAGO: They just mean we should watch our language. If I'm supposed to say to you, for example, in Act Two, Scene One, "Players in your huswifery, and huswives in your beds," should I say, Players in your huswifery and huswives in your, oh, oh, oh, oh, oh, oh?

DIRECTOR: Patience! "Two, Islamic veiling must be worn at all times."

DESDEMONA: What? Islamic veiling in a Shakespearean play?

DIRECTOR: It's not important. A scarf should solve the problem.

DESDEMONA: You mean I have to wear a head scarf even when I'm alone with my husband?

DIRECTOR: Hey, this is a theater, you know! There are going to be men in the audience. That's how things are nowadays.

"Three, the revolutionary objectives of the Islamic Republic must be fully observed at all times."

OTHELLO: Now, that takes the cake!

DIRECTOR: Oh, don't be so picky, for God's sake.

CASSIO: What do they mean by that?

DIRECTOR: They've explained it themselves. [*Pointing to IAGO*] For example, Iago has to be played as a counterrevolutionary or a plotter against the government.

IAGO: Me? Great. So tomorrow they arrest me in the street and take me to the Revolutionary Committee.

DIRECTOR: Who's going to recognize you in the street? You're going to be on stage in costume and makeup.

IAGO: But my name is going to be on the posters.

DIRECTOR: We'll use a pseudonym, ok? [*IAGO is lost in thought.*] Cassio has to be someone who's loyal to the leader of the revolution and who suffers a dark fate as a result of the plotting of counterrevolutionaries.

CASSIO: That's exactly how it is in the play.

IAGO: Yeah, people will praise your name and proclaim you a living martyr.

DESDEMONA: Would you shut up for one minute? [*To the DIRECTOR*] Shut up for one minute, ok?

DIRECTOR: "Four, half the proceeds from the ticket sales must accrue to the Martyrs' Foundation and the Center for Islamic Thought and Art."

OTHELLO: What proceeds?

DIRECTOR: They'll be in charge of everything. [*Looks at his watch. He is nervous and looks at the door.*] Look, guys, all of these problems can be solved. Don't worry. We've all worked on this play and sweated over it for months. We're not going to let these little things stop us now. But we don't have much time. In an hour, the Minister of Islamic Guidance and a representative from the Headquarters of the Cultural Revolution and a specialist in cultural affairs are supposed to come here. We ought to start getting ourselves together. [*Goes to the gunnysack, gets out several head scarves and women's Islamic dresses and gives them to DESDEMONA and EMILIA.*] You'd better make yourselves presentable. [*To DESDEMONA*] Put this on. [*Shows her a voluminous smock.*] And put this on your head. [*Gives her a scarf.*]

DESDEMONA [*astonished*]: You mean I'm supposed to be a Hezbollahi Sister? [*To EMILIA*] What do you think?

EMILIA: If you'll wear them, I'll wear them.

DESDEMONA and EMILIA put the clothing on. DESDEMONA ties her scarf and pulls it down over her forehead. They begin to chant together in the mourning tones of a Shi'ite passion play.

EMILIA and DESDEMONA:
How difficult the time when one is forlorn,
How difficult it is to be homeless and alone,
Homelessness will from our houses make us torn,
May God avenge us for the injustice shown.

The DIRECTOR is nervous. IAGO pounds on his head as though accompanying the mourners. CASSIO laughs. OTHELLO draws his sword and lunges at the DIRECTOR.

OTHELLO [*acting like a warrior in a passion play*]: O drummer, play the drums of war.

DIRECTOR [*angrily, to OTHELLO*]: You, too?

OTHELLO [*to the DIRECTOR*]: Well, what do you want me to do?

DIRECTOR: Since you're a revolutionary and a commander, you should wear a cape.

OTHELLO [*goes to a clothes rack, puts on a cape, and picks up a sword*]: To behead them all.

DIRECTOR: Do whatever you want, but don't grumble.

IAGO: What do you think I should do? [*Twirls around.*]

DIRECTOR: You just stay as you are.

CASSIO [*with a laugh, clowning*]: A counterrevolutionary can be recognized just by his face!

IAGO: Are you going to open a case against me, creep? [*Kicks at CASSIO.*]

   The set darkens.

‍CঙৎD

   The actors are rehearsing Act Three, Scene Three, scripts in hand. The DIRECTOR occasionally coaches them.

EMILIA: Madam, here comes my lord.

CASSIO: Madam, ...

DIRECTOR: Don't say it like Emilia. She talks like a lady in waiting, but you're a man, so you have to talk to her in a manly voice and not look directly at her.

CASSIO: Madam, I'll take my leave.

DIRECTOR: Skip the next two lines. [*To IAGO*] Now you.

IAGO: Hah! I like not that.

OTHELLO: What dost thou say?

IAGO: Nothing, my lord...

DIRECTOR: No, between "nothing" and "my lord" there is a pause.

IAGO: Nothing, pause, my lord.

OTHELLO: Was not that Cassio parted from my wife?

DIRECTOR: It would be better if you said that jealously.

OTHELLO: Jealously?

DIRECTOR: You're not just talking to Iago. You're addressing the whole world.

OTHELLO [*in the tone of a jealous man*]: Was not that Cassio parted from my wife?

IAGO: Cassio, my lord?

DIRECTOR: Let him go on by himself.

OTHELLO [*same tone of voice*]: I do believe 'twas he. [*The door opens suddenly and a roughneck REVOLUTIONARY GUARD bursts into the middle of the scene.*]

REVOLUTIONARY GUARD [*shouting*]: Where did he go? [*Everyone is flustered. They look at him, afraid.*]

DIRECTOR [*frightened*]: Where did who go?

REVOLUTIONARY GUARD: The one who escaped. [*Begins to sniff around in the corners.*]

DIRECTOR: Nobody has escaped, brother. We're all right here.

REVOLUTIONARY GUARD: I'm not an idiot. I heard it with my own ears, a brother said he escaped, and another brother said it was he himself. What was his name?

DIRECTOR [*with an obsequious smile*]: No, brother, we were rehearsing a play, reading it from a book. Look [*shows him a script*].

REVOLUTIONARY GUARD [*without glancing at the script, strikes it with his weapon*]: I can read, but I don't read this kind of stuff. Anyway, His Eminence and some brothers are coming here, so I've got to make sure everything is ok.

SECURITY OFFICER [*enters. Looks the room over carefully*]: Sisters and brothers, please stand apart.

REVOLUTIONARY GUARD: They stand together as though they were going to have their picture taken. [*EMILIA and DESDEMONA stand to one side and OTHELLO, IAGO, and CASSIO form another group. All are nervous and upset. For a minute the REVOLUTIONARY GUARD and the SECURITY OFFICER exit.*]

ACTORS [*to the DIRECTOR*]: Hey, what's going on?

DIRECTOR [*calmly*]: Can't you keep quiet for a little while?

ෆ৪০

A few seconds later, the MINISTER OF ISLAMIC GUIDANCE, who is a cleric, PROFESSOR KHORUSH, PROFESSOR MAKHMALCHI, and ZEYNAB SISTER enter. The actors mumble their greetings.

MINISTER: Peace and God's blessings to you. [*The DIRECTOR steps forward to arrange chairs for them.*]

DIRECTOR: Welcome, Your Honor, Your Eminence. We're so pleased you could come. Please, have a seat. [*Each of the visitors takes a chair. Only the REVOLUTIONARY GUARD and ZEYNAB SISTER remain standing.*] Your Eminence, esteemed professors, we are honored to have you here. It is very kind of you to trouble yourselves to come to our humble cultural establishment...

ZEYNAB SISTER [*interrupts*]: These sisters, why are their scarves like that? [*Steps forward. To DESDEMONA*] Put your hair under your scarf. [*To EMILIA*] You're in even worse shape. [*Pulls EMILIA's scarf down over her eyebrows, then bends over and looks at their legs.*] You're wearing sheer stockings. Cover your legs.

MINISTER: Sister, let these things wait till later. Brothers and sisters, please sit down.

    Everyone sits except the DIRECTOR, who hurries to his sack and brings out two chadors. He gives one to DESDEMONA and one to EMILIA to cover their legs with. ZEYNAB SISTER gives them a contemptuous look.

ZEYNAB SISTER [*returns to her original position*]: You seem to have forgotten all about the angels that will come to your grave to question you and punish you for your sins.

DIRECTOR [*flustered*]: Yes, it is very kind of you to visit this center of culture. We're very grateful.

MINISTER: I'm very grateful, too. I hope everyone is working toward our revolutionary goals in these centers.

PROFESSOR KHORUSH [*to the MINISTER*]: Your Reverence, these gentlemen are pious and true players of the theater who, it has been agreed, will perform a great play advancing the revolutionary goals of our Islamic Republic and who have requested the benefit of your guidance.

MINISTER: Of course, I myself am in need of guidance and advice, but I will certainly not deny you the limited scholarly resources that I possess.

PROFESSOR MAKHMALCHI [*to the MINISTER*]:   The brothers have agreed to abide by all the principles and precepts of Islamic art and the advancement of our goals. May I be so bold as to suggest that, as agreed, we carefully Islamicize the technology of the West and the East, the culture of the West and East? This work of art is a Western drama which we must adapt to Islam. God willing, with your advice, the brothers and sisters will be successful in this endeavor. [*DESDEMONA is angry. She rubs her face and a bit of her hair falls out from under her scarf.*]

ZEYNAB SISTER: Pull your scarf down, sister.

REVOLUTIONARY GUARD: These folks seem to forget that they live in an Islamic country. Maybe they think...

PROFESSOR KHORUSH [*to the REVOLUTIONARY GUARD*]:   Brother, please, His Eminence is trying to talk.

ZEYNAB SISTER: Sisters, let's go into another room while the brothers talk. Come on. [*EMILIA and DESDEMONA hesitate.*] Let's go, already. [*They exit.*]

MINISTER: In the name of God, who is ruthless to tyrants. Praise be to the leader of the people. Praise to the martyr-nurturing nation. Praise to the Guards, with their bloody shrouds. [*Little by little, he climbs up and sits on the back of the chair and puts his feet on the seat.*] We are touched by a feeling of holiness at this gathering of brothers and sisters. I hope that with the help of artists committed to our Islamic Republic, and to the displeasure of the global powers, we will day by day achieve greater victories, both on the battle ground of Islam and heathenism and on the battle front of the culture of truth against falsehood. First, let me say that the clergy have always been, are, and will always be the guardians of the trenches of war and culture through their self-sacrifice and great efforts. I should also mention that after studying the commentary of His Eminence Koleyni, with His Eminence Ayatollah Behjati— may he rest in peace—and after finishing the "Kashf al-

Morad fi Tajrid" and the "Tajrid al-E'teqad" under the late
Sheikh Ahmad Tabasi, and after a careful study of the
"Tamhid al-Qawa'ed" in the seminary at the village of
Langarud, I spent years at Haj Sheikh Mollah Ali Va'ez
Khiyabani's school in the village of Kahrizak studying the
science of drama. Thus, I am somewhat well-versed in
this Islamic subject, and I say that drama and the dramatic
arts are among the Islamic obligations and require guidelines, like all other religious affairs. To put it more simply,
full religious ablution is a religious matter which requires
guidelines. So drama, too, like full ablution, requires religious guidelines. Now, the guidelines of Islamic drama
have three principles, that is to say, three legs.

OTHELLO: Three legs?

PROFESSOR KHORUSH: Three principles.

PROFESSOR MAKHMALCHI: Three principles, that is, consisting
of three elements.

DIRECTOR: You mean, the unity of time, place, and action?

MINISTER: Sir, that is blasphemous. For example, what is the
connection between the islands of Andalusia and the end
of time? Unity should exist only among the followers.

DIRECTOR: I meant, the principles that Aristotle stated.

MINISTER: Aristo?

PROFESSOR KHORUSH: He means Aristotle.

MINISTER: Where has Stotle said that?

DIRECTOR: In his book, *The Poetics*.

MINISTER: Oh, yes, of course, you mean *The Boutiques*. I studied
it several years ago, in connection with the lectures of
Ayatollah Haj Mirza Sadeq Shemrani—God bless him. As

I recall, he talked mostly about astrolabes. He was a materialist, and my father wrote a refutation against it,
which, God willing, will be prepared for publication at an
appropriate time. When was that book written?

OTHELLO: Before Christ.

MINISTER: Yes, my own dear father referred to this matter. Since
the time of its publication was before our beloved Islam, it
is among the forbidden books, and reliance on it is not
lawful.

DIRECTOR: But, what about the three principles you mentioned?

MINISTER: I was saying that in Islamic drama, three principles
must be observed, because our drama, like our revolution,
must be exported to every part of the world. Therefore, in
the end, a true Moslem must give up his life, sacrifice his
blood, everything he has. That is, he must be one of God's
soldiers, so that the great tree of the Revolutionary Islamic
Republic is fruitful. An apostate or polytheist or, worst of
all, a Hypocrite, is punished for his evil deeds. In addition
to ransoms and fines and lashing and stoning and revolutionary execution, on Judgment Day, the fate of such
people will be revealed and become a warning and a lesson to others. Now, as to the third leg of the tripod, it is to
show repentance, how the light of faith shines in their
hearts, as a result of guardianship under the influence of
the Brothers, how they come out of prison and join the
brotherhood of the faithful. But, of course, it is necessary
in drama for the repentant to always feel humiliated, em-
barrassed, to always keep one's head lowered, to be mod-
est and contrite about one's past. And in drama, too, repentance must not be neglected. Several self-sacrificing
Guards must always watch over them so that they do not
stray from the Islamic line into the Hypocrites' groups and
establish safe houses. The late Ayatollah Baha'eddin
Qarachehdaghi in his treatise dealt with this subject several times in his short work, "Great Sins in a Small Book."

DIRECTOR: Your Eminence, all of this was contained in the letter of permission and will be carefully adhered to.

MINISTER: I come here as a seminary student for the purpose of guidance. Our brothers, the professors, have works and advice to offer. [To MAKHMALCHI] Please, give us your advice.

PROFESSOR MAKHMALCHI [shifts back and forth]: In my numerous works, I have discussed at length the techniques of fiction, poetry, drama, the cinema, photography, and religious painting. Although art stems from natural talent and is a precise and perfect observation of art, it is also a propaganda tool, one in the service of the lofty goals of the Islamic Revolution. We should ask ourselves, with the production of this play, will we move toward our lofty goals or not?

OTHELLO: This isn't a play anymore. It's the Voice and Vision of the Islamic Republic.

IAGO [punches him; quietly]: Just be patient for a minute.

OTHELLO: But the central idea of this play...

DIRECTOR: This has been discussed at length. [To MAKHMALCHI] Please, go on.

PROFESSOR MAKHMALCHI: And thus I now call on our brother, Khorush, to enlighten us.

PROFESSOR KHORUSH [rises]: In the name of God, the compassionate and the merciful, and in the name of the Creator, Who with a pen taught man learning and expression, and with praise to the holy souls of the great prophets, and with greetings to the Great Imam, may he live long and be successful, and grace to the pure blood of the martyrs of this land, I will first recite a poem, which illustrates precisely the nature of drama. A learned sage once wrote:

We are eloquent philosophically, for we are the appren-
tices of the Messiah,
Often have we taken corpses and blown into them a spirit.
We are expert physicians who take patients' urine,
Because in the body of a patient we penetrate like ideas.

Taking urine samples was a practice of the ancients in their
laboratories. Today, we would term such a sample a urine
specimen. They could diagnose a disease solely by the
sediment in urine and its color and smell. They poured
the urine of a patient into a bowl and took it to a doctor.
In a respected mystical text it is written:

I wish you were a patient and I were brown sugar,
So they would make an enema of me and put me into you.

Now, an enema is the apparatus that is inserted into the rectum
and a liquid flows into it so that a patient is treated and
cured. Therefore, in our Islamic Republic, two subjects
must be brought up. We must get urine specimens from
artists to determine what illnesses they have. [*OTHELLO
laughs loudly.*] Wait, Mr. Othello, look at the revolutionary
aspects of this matter. If we get urine samples, we won't
have artists who are supporters of the Tyrant, or Hypocrites, or Communists. It absolutely wouldn't be censorship. It's a medical procedure, so we definitely must get
samples. And brown sugar enemas, for which ancient
medical books praise their properties, stop fever, bring
psychological and spiritual health, and would bring
strength and health to our Islamic Republic. Brown sugar
enemas for the purpose of ideological-political guidance
will help us resist the global oppression of the East and
West. In the case of theater arts, they are necessary, in
other words, a responsibility.
*The actors jump up from their chairs, except for OTHELLO, who is
solemn.*

IAGO: What does this mean? They want to take urine from us?

CASSIO: I won't let them give me an enema!

REVOLUTIONARY GUARD [*raising his weapon*]:   Everyone, sit down! [*They sit.*]

MINISTER: Brothers and sisters [*notices that there are no women present*], ah, brothers, fortunately, since we are all men here, I would suggest that we note that no one has brought the necessary equipment with us. [*Reaches inside his cloak and brings out a handkerchief.*] Here it is. And these gentlemen have nothing in their briefcases except books of guidance.

DIRECTOR: I'm very grateful to the professors for their guidance, and now, if you will permit us, we will begin the rehearsal.

MINISTER: What did you say the name of the play was?

DIRECTOR: Othello.

MINISTER: Yes, yes, of course. A great writer. Of the same stature as the well-known French Islamicist, Walter. In one of his histories, maybe his "Punishments and Retributions," I read that Gustave Le Bon in his famous book, "Falamarian," greatly praised the man and rated him as among the greatest of thinkers. He wrote a book entitled [*to KHORUSH*], do you happen to recall the title?

PROFESSOR KHORUSH: Perhaps "Committed Art and Discord in Noncommitted Art." [*He quotes a few words in nonsensical English.*]

OTHELLO [*sneering*]:   Othello wasn't a writer, sir; that's the name of a play by Shakespeare.

MINISTER: That's exactly what I said. Was this Mr. Shakespeare perhaps a follower of a sacred book?

OTHELLO: He wrote plenty of plays, sir.

MINISTER: I mean, was he a monotheist?

DIRECTOR: Yes, sir, he was a Christian.

MINISTER [frowns]: So, he didn't convert to Islam?

PROFESSOR KHORUSH: Your Eminence, Shakespeare lived before the Prophet Mohammad.

MINISTER: Yes, yes, of course. God willing, in the next world, the Prophets and we Islamic scholars will intercede for him, and he will be forgiven. But what was the name of the play?

DIRECTOR: Othello!

MINISTER: In my opinion, it would be best if Shakespeare were staged.

CASSIO: Shakespeare isn't a play.

MINISTER [angry]: What difference does it make whether a playwright is staged or a play? It is contrary to our slogan, "The people must always be on the scene."

PROFESSOR MAKHMALCHI: Your Eminence, I am supposed to write a drama about this individual. But, for now, the brothers are going to act out Othello. [He calms and soothes the MINISTER.]

MINISTER: Fine. I see no problem. However, this brother Atuglu was a native of Azerbaijan, is that not correct?

OTHELLO: Azerbaijan? No, Morocco.

MINISTER: Morocco? Morocco is an Islamic country and has good relations with our Islamic and Revolutionary Republic. [KHORUSH and MAKHMALCHI nod.] If that is true, then this Christian brother Shakespeare, before the appearance of His Holiness Mohammad, had received the light of Islam in his heart, and he guided brother Otughlu—may he rest his soul. [To KHORUSH] You're learned and accomplished in this area. Why don't you enlighten us?

PROFESSOR KHORUSH: Actually, in the matter of this play, I have given a favorable opinion, because of Othello himself, who was a famous commander from the land of our brothers, Morocco, and this brother Othello, like our brother Guards, was partial to war. He continually made war, believed that war was a gift from God, a blessing from God, that it was the mission of the scholars and the prophets, that a nation was made for war, everything was made for war. Othello continually fought and believed in this divine gift and blessing.

MINISTER: So, he was a member of God's Army.

PROFESSOR MAKHMALCHI: I gave my approval to this drama for just that reason. Black Moslems were always prepared to go to war.

MINISTER: Yes, and let us not forget that Balal the Ethiopian, the Prophet's favorite muezzin, was black.

DIRECTOR: Naturally, Your Reverence, that is exactly why we chose this play. Othello's blackness is very important.

PROFESSOR MAKHMALCHI: Yes, it is very important, indeed. Permit me to make a point. [He opens his briefcase, takes out a book and thumbs through it.] In my well-known book, "Islamic Art," I discuss this point explicitly. [He finds what he is looking for.] On page 32, I say, "Hajar al-Asvad [The Stone in Mecca], round which we revolve, is black. In other words, it is the same color that has caused the oppression of a portion of humanity throughout history. For racists of all time, blackness has been vile. In our literature, too, there is no color greater than black..."

MINISTER: Then, where is this black Moslem brother who was oppressed?

DIRECTOR [*indicates OTHELLO*]: That's him.

MINISTER: Him? I have studied thoroughly the works of the late, revered Seyyed Kazem Sabzevari, who is the author of four sublime volumes, entitled "The Properties of Inanimacy," "The Properties of Animals," "The Properties of Plants," and "The Properties of Humans." In his book "The Properties of Men," he wrote that Moroccans are black. How is this brother, who is white, to portray Brother Othello, who is black?

DIRECTOR: We will make him up.

MINISTER: You'll do what?

DIRECTOR [*explaining*]: We'll paint him black.

MINISTER: God forbid! You mean you are going to interfere with God's handiwork?

PROFESSOR MAKHMALCHI: No, sir. It's colored makeup that washes off.

MINISTER: Thank God! But something has just occurred to me. Maybe all the Great Satan's black men also did that. Inform the brothers in the Nest of Spies to expose the secrets.

PROFESSOR KHORUSH: Not all of them are black, Your Reverence. As the poet said, "A Blackamoor will not come white with washing, they wash their hands and faces every day, but they never get white." They are as black as Hajar al-Asvad is black, but those black individuals among the hostages in the Nest of Spies who were freed, in my opinion, might be just like Brother Othello.

MINISTER [*slaps his knee*]: God help us! Good heavens. How careless those officials are. Before they released them, they should have taken them to a bath house and given them a good scrubbing to see if they were really black or they were Atuglus. [*To KHORUSH*] Professor, remind me to bring this point up at the next Cabinet meeting.

DIRECTOR: Could we start the rehearsal now?

MINISTER: What is the opinion of the professors?

PROFESSOR MAKHMALCHI: Yes, let's start.

ෆ⃝ඔ

The actors are on stage. The women sit on one side and the men on the other. DESDEMONA and EMILIA are in full Islamic cover. MAKHMALCHI is holding a pencil and paper. On the table in front of the MINISTER are teacups and a sugar bowl. ZEYNAB SISTER sits with DESDEMONA and EMILIA.

MINISTER: Per the principles that I have put forth, first let us see the counterrevolutionary.

DIRECTOR [*indicates IAGO*]: That's him.

REVOLUTIONARY GUARD [*suddenly draws his gun*]: Hands up!

IAGO [*flustered and frightened, raises his hands*]: Me a counterrevolutionary? Not me, during the revolution I took part in every march.

REVOLUTIONARY GUARD [*moves forward menacingly*]: What did you do during the revolution, for example?

IAGO: The same things everybody did.

REVOLUTIONARY GUARD: I broke fifty bank windows by myself, like the Imam commanded. How many did you break?

IAGO: Fifty-one.

DIRECTOR [*stepping in*]: It's true, brother, I saw him, I give you my word of honor.

REVOLUTIONARY GUARD [*to IAGO*]: How many movie theaters did you set fire to?

IAGO: Me set fire to a theater?

REVOLUTIONARY GUARD: I knew you were a counterrevolutionary.

DIRECTOR: I swear to God, he's not a counterrevolutionary.

REVOLUTIONARY GUARD [*to the DIRECTOR*]: You said he was one yourself, didn't you?

DIRECTOR: No, brother, he's imitating one.

REVOLUTIONARY GUARD: If someone imitates something, that's what he is.

PROFESSOR KHORUSH [*gets up and takes the GUARD aside*]: His file has been reviewed, brother. He's not a counterrevolutionary.

REVOLUTIONARY GUARD: Well, since you say so, fine. [*Puts his gun back in its holster, goes to his seat. To the MINISTER*] But, Your Reverence, you're a witness that I was trying to do my duty...

MINISTER [*silences him with a gesture*] Yes, brother, I saw everything. [*To the DIRECTOR, while indicating CASSIO*] This brother is one of the repentants, correct?

DIRECTOR: Correct, Your Reverence.

MINISTER: God has accepted you and the door of his mercy is open to you. [*A momentary pause; angrily*] Were you a Hypocrite before?

CASSIO [*frightened*]:   I wasn't anything, Your Reverence.   I'm a theater actor.

PROFESSOR MAKHMALCHI: What His Reverence means is, in your role, what kind of beliefs do you have?

CASSIO: I'm Cassio. [*To the director*] What beliefs do I have?

PROFESSOR MAKHMALCHI: That is, before you played the role of Cassio, who is one of the repentants, what beliefs did you have?

DIRECTOR: In the beginning of the play, Iago describes your character perfectly. [*To IAGO*] Brother, read that part for us.

IAGO [*flips through a script and reads from the middle of a dialog*]:   But he...

DIRECTOR [*to the MINISTER and PROFESSORS*]:   He means him [*indicating CASSIO*].

IAGO: But he (as loving his own pride and purposes)
         Evades them with a bumbast circumstance
         Horribly stuff'd with epithets of war,
         And...

MINISTER: What kind of repentance is this?

DIRECTOR: A counterrevolutionary is speaking these words, Your Reverence. Excuse me. [*To IAGO*] Lower down, a few lines below that.

IAGO [*searches and finds the place*]:   For sooth, a great arithmetician,
         One Michael Cassio, a Florentine.
         [*Mumbles through a few more lines.*]
         Mere prattle without practice
         Is all his soldiership.

MINISTER [*happy*]: That's very true. From what he says you must be one of the repentant, but you must forget about the past completely. I hope the temptations of God's enemies won't lead you astray. [*To the DIRECTOR*] Now, what about these sisters? Who are they?

DIRECTOR [*indicates DESDEMONA*]:   Desdemona is Othello's wife. [*Indicates OTHELLO.*]

MINISTER: His legal wife?

DIRECTOR: Yes, sir, with full benefit of clergy.

REVOLUTIONARY GUARD: God bless them.

MINISTER: And this other sister? [*Indicates EMILIA.*]

DIRECTOR: She's the legal wife of Brother Iago.

MINISTER: What was the name of this brother?

DIRECTOR: Cassio.

MINISTER: And is this Brother Casico married?

DIRECTOR: No, sir, he has a lover... [*suddenly realizes what he has said, claps his hand over his mouth, then continues calmly*]...by the name of Bianca, who unfortunately is not present for this rehearsal.

MINISTER [*distressed and confused*]: A lover?

ZEYNAB SISTER [*shouting*]: It's obvious why she isn't here.

REVOLUTIONARY GUARD: The Bureau of Moral Turpitude will deal with her.

DIRECTOR: Sir, this is a Western play.

MINISTER [*angrily*]: In an Islamic country, having a lover and that sort of thing is against the law. In fact, it is promotion of debauchery. [*To the PROFESSORS*] This document should be reviewed by the Bureau. The Ministry of Guidance cannot make a decision on this alone.

REVOLUTIONARY GUARD: Do you want me to call them?

PROFESSOR KHORUSH: Call whom?

REVOLUTIONARY GUARD: His Reverence Ehya'eddin. He could send someone over.

MINISTER: To do what?

REVOLUTIONARY GUARD: To take this adulterer to the Bureau.

DIRECTOR [*flustered, pleading*]: Professor, couldn't you explain...

PROFESSOR MAKHMALCHI [*to the GUARD*]: Brother, it's just play-acting; it will be completely Islamic. Please, be patient.

CASSIO [*taking the director aside*]: I for one am not prepared to act. I'm serious. On the one hand, I have to be one of the repentant, on the other hand, they brand me an adulterer. [*To the MINISTER*] Sir, I have a wife and children. I lead a respectable life.

MINISTER: Then, why have you taken a lover?

CASSIO: Who says I've taken a lover? That's in the play.

DIRECTOR [*flustered*]: Allow me, Your Eminence, to submit that we have thought of this previously, because obviously the existence of a lover is against Islamic law, so we have decided to completely cut the lover out of the play and have Bianca played by Cassio's lawful wife.

CASSIO: But my wife isn't an actress.

DIRECTOR [*gritting his teeth*]:   In the play, she's your legal wife. Why don't you listen? [*The door opens and BIANCA, who is taking off her scarf, enters, not noticing the others.*]

BIANCA: I'm really sorry, but... [*Reties her scarf when she sees who is present. The MINISTER and his retinue look at her angrily.*]

MINISTER: And who would this sister be?

DIRECTOR [*troubled*]: Bianca.

ZEYNAB SISTER: Uh huh, they think our heads are empty. But as a revolutionary woman, I know what's going on here. Bianca means "bi-nikah," unmarried, whore. [*She spits on the floor.*]

REVOLUTIONARY GUARD: Yeah, they themselves said "lover."

ZEYNAB SISTER [*to BIANCA*]: Cover yourself properly. [*Gets up and pulls BIANCA's scarf down over her forehead.*]

OTHELLO [*to the DIRECTOR, angrily*]:   Let's forget this whole thing. Let's forget about plays. Who needs plays?

MINISTER: No, no, no, as the brother professor said [*indicates MAKHMALCHI*], we need art, we love and respect it. You are obliged to produce this play as a religious duty, but everything must be in accordance with Islamic law.

DIRECTOR: Nothing contrary to religious law has occurred, Your Reverence.

MINISTER: In any case, I think there is a simple remedy for this problem. I'll marry this woman and this man temporarily, right now, and we can go on from there. [*He recites the formula for a temporary marriage and takes from the sugar bowl a lump of sugar, breaks it in two, and gives one piece to BIANCA and the other piece to CASSIO.*] Congratulations. [*BIANCA and CASSIO look at each other. CASSIO throws his piece on the floor.*]

BIANCA [*to the DIRECTOR*]: I came by to say I can't be in this
  play, and I apologize, that's all. [*Throws her lump of sugar
  on the floor and exits.*]

ZEYNAB SISTER [*shouting*]: Yes, get back to your real job. She
  thinks we can't get her!

REVOLUTIONARY GUARD [*to CASSIO*]: Can't you control your
  wife?

DIRECTOR [*to the MINISTER*]: Shall we start the rehearsal now?

MINISTER: Go ahead.

DIRECTOR: In any case, Sister Bianca is dropped, and now we'll
  run through a part that the brothers and sisters will act out
  in accordance with religious law. Let's start with Act Two,
  Scene Three. [*To the MINISTER*] In this scene, we're in
  Othello's palace.

MINISTER: Not "palace," dear sir, "ghetto," by order of Imam
  Khomeyni. Remember the words of the Imam, "the palace
  dwellers are vanquished and the ghetto-dwellers are victorious."

DIRECTOR: Yes, I'm very sorry. We're now in Othello's ghetto-
  dwelling, in a grand hall in Othello's ghetto-dwelling.
  There is furniture here and there, handwoven carpets on
  the floors, and chandeliers hanging from the ceiling.
  Brother Othello, Sister Desdemona, and Brother Cassio are
  on stage. [*Points to each one.*] Ok, let's start. [*The actors
  clear their throats.*]

OTHELLO [*to CASSIO*]: Good Michael, look you to the guard
  tonight.
  Let's teach ourselves that honorable stop
  Not to outsport discretion.

CASSIO: Iago hath direction what to do;
  But notwithstanding, with my personal eye

Will I look to't.

OTHELLO: Iago is most honest.
Michael, good night. Tomorrow with your earliest
Let me have speech with you. Come, my dear love...

MINISTER: My dear what?

OTHELLO: My dear love.

MINISTER [to the DIRECTOR]:   Aren't these two characters
supposed to be married?

DIRECTOR: Certainly, Your Reverence, I mentioned that before.

MINISTER: Does anyone call his wife "my dear love"?

OTHELLO: Then what are we supposed to say?

MINISTER: Sir, that's Western and morally corrupt. We refer to
our wives as "spouse," "privates," "weakling," "woman of
the house."

OTHELLO: But that isn't what it says in the script.

MINISTER: So what? It has to say something that will not en-
flame the people with lust.

OTHELLO [to DESDEMONA, angrily]: Come, my woman of the
house, the purchase made, the fruits are to ensue...

MINISTER: So, Brother Atuglu is an honorable merchant, in
addition to being a commander?

DIRECTOR: No, Your Reverence, they are just talking about the
daily affairs of the country. [Explains] At this point,
Brother Othello and Sister Desdemona exit and brother
Cassio is left by himself on the stage. Then Brother Iago
enters.

CASSIO [to IAGO]: Welcome, Iago. We must to the watch.

IAGO: Not this hour, brother, sir...

PROFESSOR KHORUSH: "Brother," just brother.

IAGO: Not this hour, Brother; 'tis not yet ten o'th'clock. Our general cast us thus early for the love of his Desdemona; who let us not therefore blame. He hath not yet made wanton the night with her; and she is sport for Jove.

CASSIO: She's a most exquisite lady.

IAGO: And I'll warrant her, full of game.

CASSIO: Indeed, she's a most fresh and delicate creature.

IAGO: What an eye she has! Methinks it sounds a parley to provocation.

MINISTER [*to the PROFESSORS*]: I don't understand. This place is a den of fornication and corruption and adultery.

PROFESSOR MAKHMALCHI [*gets up*]: I completely agree with His Eminence. Let me point out just a few things. Brother Iago says, "He has not yet made wanton the night with her." [*To IAGO, threateningly*] How do you know that? Were you in their bedroom? Yes, or no?

IAGO: I swear to God I wasn't in anybody's bedroom.

PROFESSOR MAKHMALCHI: Then how did you know that?

OTHELLO: Shakespeare has used this point intentionally for Iago to make Cassio jealous about Desdemona.

PROFESSOR MAKHMALCHI: This brother, in addition to spreading prostitution, is also a middleman and a pimp.

IAGO: What are you saying, sir? I've retired from a life as a teacher, and I've been interested in acting and the theater for years. So such accusations won't stick to me.

DIRECTOR: The professor doesn't mean you, he means Iago.

IAGO: Aren't I Iago?

DIRECTOR: You're Iago in the play; outside the play, it's obvious who you are. You're not a bastard like Iago.

REVOLUTIONARY GUARD: So he's a bastard, too.

MINISTER: Brother, let us see where it all leads to. [*To IAGO*] Go on.

IAGO [*to CASSIO*]:   Come lieutenant,
I have a jug of wine, and without are a brace of Cyprus gallants...

REVOLUTIONARY GUARD [*intrudes suddenly*]: Aha! A jug of wine? Where is this jug?

DIRECTOR: No, Brother, he said "without are a brace of Cyprus gallants..."

REVOLUTIONARY GUARD: I don't understand this stuff. Where's the jug?

DIRECTOR [*pleading*]: There's no jug involved. They've drunk wine in the drama.

REVOLUTIONARY GUARD: It makes no difference to me where they drank it, Cafe Deram, Cafe Kowkab, Aqa Reza Soheyla, whatever. [*Goes to OTHELLO.*] Go "huuuh."

OTHELLO [*reluctantly and forcefully*]: Huh.

REVOLUTIONARY GUARD: What kind of a "huuuh" is that? Are you a bellows?

OTHELLO: That's how I go "huh."

REVOLUTIONARY GUARD [*goes to CASSIO*]: Go "huuuh."
CASSIO: Huh.

REVOLUTIONARY GUARD [*to IAGO*]: You've definitely drunk some. But then it's impossible for a counterrevolutionary not to have drunk some. [*IAGO withdraws and resists.*]

DIRECTOR [*to the MINISTER*]: Your Eminence, these brothers and sisters aren't the sort to indulge in alcoholic beverages, carousing, and that sort of thing.

MINISTER: Brother director, I can't interfere in the brother Guard's execution of his revolutionary duties. It would be contrary to the law. It is true they haven't drunk anything, but it is advisable that they go "huh."

REVOLUTIONARY GUARD [*to IAGO, who is backing up and resistant*]: Are you trying to get away? Open up and go "huuuh."

DIRECTOR: Don't be afraid, brother, go "huh" and get it over with. [*IAGO goes "huh."*]

REVOLUTIONARY GUARD: It's true, I don't like that black guy, but to be fair, he does good huhing. Now it's the sisters' turn.

ZEYNAB SISTER [*steps forward, to DESDEMONA*]: Cover your face and open your mouth. [*DESDEMONA goes "huh."*] Ooo! What a smell these Westernized types give off. [*To EMILIA*] Your turn. [*EMILIA goes "huh."*] They haven't drunk anything, so far...

OTHELLO [*to the DIRECTOR*]: Enough. Let's give up. To hell with theater and Shakespeare and acting. This isn't the way to produce a play. We've had it.

GUARD AND ZEYNAB SISTER: Shut up and sit down.

DIRECTOR [*flustered, pleading to the MINISTER*]: Your Eminence, I beg you, could we be excused from this play?

MINISTER: No, sir, no. It's actually very important. This is how we can prevent corruption. Note that a Committee has been formed, composed of the faithful and committed members of the Ministry of Guidance and the Bureau of Prohibitions, to deal with these issues carefully. And I am very pleased that the work of these brothers is so precise. I ask Brother Professor Khorush to express his views.

PROFESSOR KHORUSH: I think that Brother Professor Makhmalchi should give us his views.

PROFESSOR MAKHMALCHI: In my view, this scene must be absolutely omitted, because as playwrighting, it is deficient in spiritual value and divine esthetics.

OTHELLO: In other words, we should bury the play right here and just wash our hands of it?

PROFESSOR KHORUSH: No, no, not at all. What is meant is to observe our revolutionary policies and cultural values. Other than that, we have nothing in mind. Your Reverence, please, don't be angry. Note that all of this must be deleted and rewritten, and, God willing, that will be done. I have an amended proposal. It would be advisable to rehearse the last part of the play, which is in conformity with Islamic standards and moral principles. [To the MINISTER] What is your opinion?

MINISTER [knitting his brow]: I have no objection. Actually, I've read that His Holiness Sadeq has been reported to say it is better to start a drama from the end. In fact, as the saying goes, "What do they do with the chicks after they hatch?"

OTHELLO [sarcastically]: They count them and eat them. [The MINISTER laughs, then the PROFESSORS laugh, and the GUARD laughs.]

PROFESSOR MAKHMALCHI: Of course, in my works I show the deepest respect and admiration for the character of Shakespeare, whose name and works have been distorted and

misrepresented by the world imperialism. Right now, I'm
in the midst of writing a book in which I prove that Shakespeare was a Moslem Bedouin Arab by the name of
Sheykh Zobeyr, whose name and works have been distorted and continue to be distorted, and in my extensive
research, I've reached the conclusion that the martyred
Sheykh Zobeyr in one of his other works, *Romeo and Juliet*,
originally Rahim and Raheleh, shows that their love for
one another increases after they are legally married. It is
their families, who do not oppose their courting or moral
corruption, who really cause this tragedy.

MINISTER: Bravo. You are absolutely correct.

DIRECTOR [*to MAKHMALCHI*]: What do you say about Othello?

PROFESSOR MAKHMALCHI: In my research, which I hope will
soon be published, I address this question. The editing of
this drama must be based on divine aesthetics, because it
contains important points about chastity and the sanctity
of the family, which are obligatory for Moslems.

OTHELLO: So, now what are we supposed to do?

PROFESSOR KHORUSH: Excuse me, Brother Othello. With no
offense to the great poet Hafez, who memorized the entire
Koran, Shakespeare can be considered the Hafez of his
time. For centuries people have resolved their problems
through faith in divination using Hafez's poetry. Now we
should practice divination with drama to see what Shakespeare tells us. I will ask His Eminence to be so kind as to
perform the divination. [*Takes the DIRECTOR's script from
him and gives it to the MINISTER. The MINISTER closes his
eyes and in the style of a fortuneteller, opens the script at random.*]

MINISTER: "In sleep I heard him, 'Sweet Desdamama.'" [*To
KHORUSH*] Desdamama?

PROFESSOR KHORUSH: No, Your Eminence, it's "Desdemona."

MINISTER: Whatever. He said, "Sweet Desdamama. Let us be
    wary, let us hide our loves." [*To the DIRECTOR*] I don't
    understand. Are these two husband and wife?

DIRECTOR: He was dreaming.

MINISTER: Damn the devil. [*Adjusts his glasses and reads*]

> "And then, sir, would he gripe and wring my hand;
> Cry, 'O sweet creature!'"
> It is shameful, sir. It is true that the clerics must discuss all
> matters, but "O sweet creature"...?

PROFESSOR KHORUSH: Your Eminence, it's just a figure of
    speech. The Tongue of the Unknown, Hafez, used many
    of these mystical and divine metaphors. For example, he
    says:

> Pardon me if the string of prayer beads broke,
> I was holding the silvery white arm of the cup-bearer.

> The silvery white arm of the beloved is an allusion to
> spiritual grace.

MINISTER: So it was a mystical matter?

PROFESSOR KHORUSH: That's right, Your Reverence.

MINISTER: Correct...

> "Then he kissed me hard,
> As if..." [*Pauses.*]

> But this is not mystical. His Eminence Professor Ja'fari, in
> his book, "Discovering Mysticism," in Makshuf al-Loghat
> said, "kissing has no metaphorical meaning in the world of
> mysticism. [*He closes the script and tosses it on the table.*]

PROFESSOR KHORUSH: Your Eminence, please, don't be angry; I will retract my suggestion. I would suggest instead that they rehearse a part of the last scene of the play.

MINISTER: I have no objection. Let's count from the end.

PROFESSOR MAKHMALCHI [*laughs*]: In both modern and ancient science, it was customary to count backwards.

DIRECTOR [*to the actors*]: Friends...

REVOLUTIONARY GUARD [*with a shout*]: "Friends"? That's communist. You should say "brothers and sisters."

DIRECTOR [*with a respectful smile, to the GUARD*]: Excuse me. [*To the actors*] Brothers and sisters, let's rehearse the last part, so that, God willing, we can put this play on at last...

OTHELLO: Let's go in reverse gear to get to the beginning.

PROFESSOR MAKHMALCHI: Brother Othello, please remember that the structure of an Islamic drama requires true spirituality and complete contemplation and profitable mediation and help us reach our revolutionary goals, that is, we must understand that a peach pit is really a peach pit in order to eat the peach.

OTHELLO: But until you've eaten the peach, you can't see the pit.

PROFESSOR MAKHMALCHI: Revolutionary art, sir, must above all consider political and ideological content. The edible part of the peach itself is not a consideration. On page 104 of my book, I suggest that, in the writer's words, whatever is not necessary and has no role in the general progress of a story must not be used. What do I mean by progress? What? The pit of the peach. The ideological-political pit of the issues.

OTHELLO: So the only value of a peach is its pit?

PROFESSOR MAKHMALCHI [*to the GUARD*]: Brother, make him be quiet.

REVOLUTIONARY GUARD: Shut up, already. Let the brother professor speak.

PROFESSOR MAKHMALCHI: Since an Islamic story or drama is Islamic art, whatever is contrary to the views of Islamic law and morality must be discarded. Do you understand, Brother Othello?

OTHELLO [*shouting*]: No, I don't understand.

PROFESSOR KHORUSH [*mediates*]: If you will permit me, I will make a brief explanation. In the Koranic chapter, "Al-Safat," I think it is Verse 6, where it states, "We adorn the sky of the world with stars," what is meant is a kind of precise aesthetics. In committed Islamic art, the small stars that we see are in fact the pits, which, according to Brother Makhmalchi, are the pits of the peach.

OTHELLO: Then, why don't they have branches and leaves and flowers and fruit?

REVOLUTIONARY GUARD: Shut up, already. Don't get yourself in trouble. [*OTHELLO stays quiet with a half smile.*]

DIRECTOR: Professor, please give your guidance in a summary fashion.

PROFESSOR KHORUSH: Yes, well, my apologies, I think that the professor's view is correct, that we should see where it all ends.

DIRECTOR: Fine. [*To the actors*] Sisters and brothers...

REVOLUTIONARY GUARD: What? You're supposed to say "brothers and sisters."

DIRECTOR [*to the GUARD*]:   Sorry. Brothers and sisters, let's rehearse the last part, so that, God willing, with the permit that has been issued previously, we will rehearse the play and prepare it for *mise en scéne.*

REVOLUTIONARY GUARD: Miss who?

DIRECTOR: *mise en scéne.*

PROFESSOR KHORUSH: That means they don't just sit, they get up and get moving.

REVOLUTIONARY GUARD: Get moving? Do they want to have a march?

PROFESSOR KHORUSH: No, brother, it means they can move around the stage.

REVOLUTIONARY GUARD [*plays with his gun*]: I know that, but His Reverence in the Committee has said that...

MINISTER: I'll explain it to His Reverence myself, don't worry.

DIRECTOR: Professors, shall we begin now?

OTHELLO: We should finish it.

PROFESSOR MAKHMALCHI: Brother Othello, we're just getting into the matter. The rehearsal definitely must be continued.

DIRECTOR: Very well, Brother. [*To the actors*] Brothers and sisters, we should rehearse some parts of Act Two, Scene Five, that are at the end of the play. [*To OTHELLO*] Please, Brother Othello, do this part with complete composure, as though an audience were present.

OTHELLO: Fine. [*Pauses for a second to get himself ready and speaks in a serious tone*]

It is the cause, it is the cause, my soul.
Let me not name it to you, you chaste stars!
It is the cause. Yet I'll not shed her blood,
Nor scar that whiter skin of hers than snow
And smooth as monumental alabaster.
Yet she must die, else...

PROFESSOR MAKHMALCHI: Wait. Your Eminence, what is
    your opinion?

MINISTER: I can't make any sense out of it.

PROFESSOR KHORUSH: This woman [indicates DESDEMONA]
    has betrayed her husband and he wants to take her life.

MINISTER: Could you repeat that once again?

OTHELLO: It is the cause, it is the cause, my soul.

MINISTER: We know the rest, just repeat the ending.

OTHELLO [flustered]: Yet I'll not shed her blood,
    Nor scar that whiter skin of hers than snow
    And smooth as monumental alabaster.
    Yet she must die...

MINISTER: Bravo. She must die. But in my humble opinion, this
    is how it should be performed. [He gets up and goes Center
    Stage, and in the style of a villain in a religious passion play
    says]

    Oh, this whore is still here.
    Surely she should be killed,
    To guard the seed of our religion.
    Kill her now in the name of our religion.

    [To KHORUSH and MAKHMALCHI] What is the opinion of
    you learned scholars?

PROFESSOR MAKHMALCHI: I have expressed the same view in my research.

MINISTER: But, how should she die?

DIRECTOR: Brother Othello, please do that part about the praying.

OTHELLO: Have you prayed tonight, Desdemona?

DESDEMONA: Aye, my lord.

OTHELLO: If you bethink yourself of any crime
Unreconciled as yet to heaven and grace,
Solicit for it straight.

MINISTER [*to KHORUSH*]: Don't these Christians ask for salvation after praying?

REVOLUTIONARY GUARD: Hypocrites don't understand about these things. [*The SECURITY OFFICER enters, goes toward the MINISTER, points to his watch.*]

MINISTER [*looks at his watch*]: Brothers, let us be brief, since I have to attend a Cabinet meeting concerning sending troops to the front.

DIRECTOR [*quickly*]: The murder scene, the murder scene.

OTHELLO: By heaven, I saw my handkerchief in 's hand.

REVOLUTIONARY GUARD: If he saw it, he saw it.

MINISTER [*gets up*]: A handkerchief isn't right. It has various meanings in religious books, and since this adulterous woman has just prayed, it must have been her prayer rug she gave to Brother Casico.

OTHELLO: By heaven, I saw my prayer rug which I had given you in Cassio's hand.

PROFESSOR MAKHMALCHI: That's wrong dramatically. No one carries a prayer rug around.

OTHELLO [*angry, crazed*]: By heaven, I saw with my own eyes Cassio praying on the rug I gave you.

MINISTER [*in a loud voice*]: I said before that we must be careful about these Repentants. First they commit adultery on a rug, and then they pray on it. [*Spits.*]

PROFESSOR KHORUSH: Your Eminence, this part is beneficial to our revolution, and using it would expose the Hypocrites.

MINISTER: Well, what's after this?

DIRECTOR: Summarize, summarize.

DESDEMONA: Kill me to-morrow.

OTHELLO: Nay, an' you strive...

DESDEMONA: But half an hour! While I say one prayer.

OTHELLO: It is too late.

MINISTER: Wait, brothers. An adulteress must be punished in accordance with Islamic law. Her husband may be indigent and unable to pay a fine, and under Islamic law the woman must then be stoned.

DESDEMONA: Stoned?

MINISTER [*calmly*]: Yes. It is one of the laws of punishment of the Islamic Republic.

DESDEMONA [*angry*]: On stage?

MINISTER: Where else? People must see it and draw a lesson.

DESDEMONA: But I...

DIRECTOR: Sister Desdemona, please be patient. In the production, I'll arrange everything.

DESDEMONA [*shouts*]: But I haven't done anything.

MINISTER: Don't be upset, woman. If you have committed a sin, you must be punished for your act, and if not, in the next world you will thrive and live among the angels, and you'll be one of God's martyrs. An adulteress must receive punishment for her crime. Let it be a lesson to us all. [*He rises to leave.*]

PROFESSOR KHORUSH: Your Eminence, please watch this part, too. We'll get there on time. Please rehearse that section with Sister Emilia and Brother Othello.

OTHELLO: 'Tis pitiful; but yet Iago knows
That she with Cassio hath the act of shame
A thousand times committed. Cassio confessed it...

MINISTER [*to the PROFESSORS*]: So, besides the delightful issue of adultery, there is the fascinating discussion of sodomy.

DIRECTOR: No, sir, the issue is dramatic plot.

MINISTER: That's what I said. To commit mortal sins they first make a plot and then engage in conspiracy. [*Looks at his watch.*] Brothers and sisters, I don't have much time left. [*To EMILIA*] This sister, Om-e Leyla, you said...

DIRECTOR: Emilia, Your Eminence.

MINISTER: That's what I meant. Om-e Leyla. You said she's the wife of this brother, Yahoo, God bless them. But I wanted to know how she would appear in the revolutionary role of the drama.

DIRECTOR: Sister Emilia, please do that section at the end of your part.

EMILIA: What did thy song bode, lady?

Hark, canst thou hear me?

OTHELLO: I have another weapon in this chamber;
It is a sword of Spain, the ice-brook's temper.

PROFESSOR MAKHMALCHI: I object. This kind of talk is that of
Hypocrites. They have songs. "Canst thou hear" is a code.
The weapon in the brook is an allusion to a guerilla op-
eration.

OTHELLO: This was written several centuries ago. What does it
have to do with guerilla operations?

MINISTER: Yes, the seeds of discord were sown in those days.
Islam was hindered by the Hypocrites right from the be-
ginning. The Hypocrites are worse than infidels, the Great
Satan. Satan has existed from the beginning of time. The
Great Satan means these ideas. It means rejecting. [*To
KHORUSH*] What do they call it?

PROFESSOR KHORUSH: Code.

MINISTER: Yes, coat.

PROFESSOR KHORUSH: Meaning, to talk in code, secretly, with
signs.

MINISTER: No, sir, this play, Mr. Othello, or whatever, which
pretends to be Islamic, definitely has had contact with
world imperialism, even international Zionism.

REVOLUTIONARY GUARD: Your Eminence, if you want, I can
phone the Nest of Spies right now and they'll bring the
documents about this guy, Othello.

PROFESSOR KHORUSH: Brother, he's been dead a long time.

REVOLUTIONARY GUARD: What do you mean, he's dead? This
counterrevolutionary guy is sitting here saying he's
Othello. He said it a hundred times. The evidence is ready

and waiting in the Nest of Spies.   The Revolutionary
Court's duty is to put these Hotellos and Motellos and Ya-
hoos and Ahoos against the wall. I'm ready to shoot him
myself and fill him full of holes.

PROFESSOR KHORUSH: Allow me, allow me. At this point, it is
imperative that Professor Makhmalchi give his opinion, to
certainly change it. That is, it should be given a divine,
spiritual framework, which, as Professor Ja'fari says, goes
beyond the surface and the visible. And, by the grace of
God, it becomes grafted or, according to the martyr of the
altar, Professor Dastgheyb, God rest his soul, assume a
new form. In other words, eliminating all the opponents
of the Islamic Republic. Secondly, changing the content so
that in ideological-political terms it would be harmonious.
That is to say, our beloved Islam can resolve many of the
problems of the downtrodden in the world with its
beauty.

OTHELLO: Yes, it is unfortunate..., but...

EMILIA: Oh.

IAGO: Hold your peace.

EMILIA: 'Twill out; 'twill out! I peace?
No, I will speak as liberal as the north.

REVOLUTIONARY GUARD: That's what you think. I'll take you
in to the Committee.

EMILIA: Let heaven and men and devils, let them all,
All, all, cry shame against me, yet...

REVOLUTIONARY GUARD: Shut up, you...

DIRECTOR: Permit me. [To OTHELLO] Do the last part.

OTHELLO [goes off, then enters with a candlestick, goes toward
DESDEMONA]

I kissed thee ere I killed thee, No way but this,
Killing myself, to die upon a kiss.

PROFESSOR MAKHMALCHI: This is not good drama. Explain to
them, Your Eminence.

MINISTER: What can I say? In the interpretation of "Al-Manj," by
the late Haj Molla Kashi, may he rest in peace, we read
about fornication with the dead, even one's spouse. The
adulterer and adulteress will end up in the lower part of
hell, where everything is ice and fire, and the wretches
will be roasted to feed snakes. [Stands facing the professors.]
No sir, this seemingly Islamic play, Mr. Atuglu, is connected with global oppressors and international Zionism.
[Referring to the actors and DIRECTOR] These are the
sworn enemies of the Islamic Republic. [To the SECURITY
OFFICER] Brother Abbasi, tell the brother guards to
watch these people until appropriate decisions have been
made. [Motioning to MAKHMALCHI and KHORUSH]
Let's go, gentlemen.

OTHELLO [shouts]: Soft you; a word or two before you go.

REVOLUTIONARY GUARD: Get this Brother Atillo. He thinks
we are still in the Tyrant's era. Well, a Revolutionary
Court will decide.

MINISTER [interrupts GUARD]: Brother, the door to holy salvation is open to everyone. This brother may want to join
the Repentants.

OTHELLO [theatrically]: And say besides that in Aleppo once,
Where a malignant and a turbaned Turk
Beat a Venetian and traduced the state,
I took by th' throat the circumcised dog
And smote him, thus.
    He takes IAGO's sword from its scabbard and attacks the
    MINISTER. The lights go on and off

Mirror -Polishing Storytellers

Personae:

MASTER ABBAS (FIRST STORYTELLER)
MASTER BORZU (SECOND STORYTELLER)
MASTER GHOLAMHOSEYN GHULBACHEH
JAMAL'S FATHER
JAMAL
JAMAL'S MOTHER
ESMA'IL'S FATHER
ESMA'IL'S MOTHER
ESMA'IL
CLERIC
VENDER
IMAM OF THE AGE
FIRST IRAQI SOLDIER
SECOND IRAQI SOLDIER

1

In front of the curtain the FIRST STORYTELLER appears. At the
same time, we hear several loud drum beats. The FIRST
STORYTELLER paces back and forth several times in bewil-
derment and looks at the audience with surprise. He stops and
stares, puzzled, at one of the spectators.

FIRST STORYTELLER: Why are you looking at me like that? I
    don't have any tricks up my sleeve in my work. I tell all.
    That's how I am, Uncle. [*Shows his empty hands*] Have I
    grown hair on my palms? Then I would have a trick up
    my sleeve. But no, today's storyteller polishes his mir-
    ror, bares all; he breaks through the skin and exposes the
    veins and nerves, the wounds of the soul, the heart's
    blood. Today's storyteller is a mirror polisher, and today
    we've placed the mirror in such a way as to reveal to you
    a large picture of the greatest of calamities.

Exits. SECOND STORYTELLER enters suddenly from another
direction and shouts.

SECOND STORYTELLER: War! Senseless, absurd, but not
    without cause and reason. The means of war are the
    most expensive products in the world. One party makes
    them, sells them and makes a profit, while another party
    buys them and engages in death and destruction, and so
    gains a foothold on a position of power. [*Smirking*] Yes,
    if there weren't any dead in the equation, the hearse
    drivers and corpse washers and grave diggers, eulogists
    and prayer leaders couldn't earn their daily bread. It's
    not without reason that workers in the shrouding and
    burial businesses always keep their eyes on the gates of
    the cemeteries. Corpses, cadavers, the dead--if they
    come, the workers' side dishes at dinner will be thicker
    and richer. [*Pauses for a moment, then loudly*] But, oh, the

day that the corpse washers, grave diggers, and prayer leaders reach a position of power and sit on the throne! [*He is silent, walks back and forth a few times, then suddenly stops and pretends to have a gun in his hand. He addresses a spectator.*] What's this? [*To another spectator*] Don't you know what it is? It's a gun. You can call it anything you want, M1, G3, Uzi, Kalashnikov. [*To another spectator*] What is it made of? Wood and iron. [*To himself*] Goodness, such things they can make and have made out of wood and iron. [*To another spectator*] Each of them has several parts. Look, this is called the stock; this is the barrel; this is the loader; and this is the trigger. [*Very quickly and seriously*] Now wait, while I load a bullet. [*Pretends to load a bullet, then aims the imaginary gun at various places in the audience.*] Which of you should I shoot? [*Aims carefully at someone in the back of the audience and pulls the trigger. We hear the frightening sound of a shot.*] One person killed. [*Puts the imaginary gun aside, stretches, takes a deep breath and suddenly moves his right arm up and down as if weighted and says*] What's this one? It's called a .45 caliber. They used to call it an elephant gun. It's very heavy. It can't be easily aimed. You just lift it and as it lines up with the target... [*The loud, deep sound of a shot is heard.*] Another one killed. [*Assumes the air of a war hero and jumps to one side, gets on his knees and pretends to load a clip in a heavy machine gun. Closes one eye and the sound of machine gun fire fills the theater. He gets up and brushes himself off.*] Twenty-three people sent to their deaths with a heavy machine gun. [*Kindly*] Don't be afraid. None of you has died, yet. And now, look! [*Makes a fist*] What do you think I've got in my hand? An apple? A pear? A peach, an orange, a tangerine? No, none of those. It's a grenade. [*Pulls the pin on the grenade and tosses it into the audience. We hear a terrific explosion, shouts and wailing. Silence for a moment. He paces and looks all around himself, then stares at the sky and says with a smile*] My goodness gracious, what a pretty bird! How fast it flies. It's coming closer. It looks strange. It doesn't flap its wings, and it seems to be made of silver. Now it's laying an egg in the air. [*Sound of a bomb explod-*

ing and the screaming and shouting of people fleeing, then the sound of falling debris, etc. Our STORYTELLER lies down on the ground as though dead. The noise subsides and he gets up. Tired and beat, he limps toward an exit.] No, no, for now I'll skip chemical warfare. I don't want the human species to become extinct all at once. For now, colts, grenades, tanks, bombs, bullets, machine guns, clubs, chains, crowbars, flamethrowers, and so forth and so on, are enough. They kill so many! [*Exits behind the curtain. Silence for a moment. The FIRST STORYTELLER enters.*]

FIRST STORYTELLER [*shakes his head sadly*]: It seems our dear friend has lost his mind and has forgotten what story telling is all about and what a storyteller is. A story is a story, and a storyteller is someone who reveals the secrets behind the curtain. A storyteller, with thousands of tricks, sometimes with a comforting, happy song, and sometimes with a sad, depressing moan, draws people out of their houses and homes. But what can you do? Today, no one is that crazy. No, the old times have not become new. But everyone's wings have been clipped. Remember the good old times, when we used to sit by the fire at night and listen to the stories of the famous Amir Arsalan, the lion-catching Shiruyeh, and the Book of Rostam? But today, there are storytellers who fabricate lies and have made everyone miserable. But no one listens to their stories. No one credits their story telling.

When the storyteller strikes all with a sword
Then no one can escape the power of his word.

[*He pauses for a moment and then, smiling*] Don't be sad, oh heart! Even though many have retreated into solitude, hearts have not broken away from each other. [*Suddenly comes forward and speaks in a sincere tone.*] By the way, do you remember Gholamhoseyn Ghulbacheh? I don't think so. He was the master of all of us storytellers who hold our lives in the palm of our hands. He never accepted servitude to anyone. I wish you had heard him tell the story of the death of Sohrab. [*Pauses*] Death of

Sohrab! Yes, the killing of the son at the hand of the father, the young at the hand of the old, the young mind at
the hand of the old mind.

Nimbly from his waste he drew out his blade
A slash to the side of his young son he made.

When the old mind rides on the back of the young mind, the
new generation must either stand before the firing squad
or go to the battle front. In any case, the bellies of all
these budding young men must be rent.

Hasten to see what end Sohrab will meet
For the land of Iran, now we must weep.

Gholamhoseyn Ghulbacheh, the sad and enlightened
mourner, lamented the killing of the young all his life
and poured dust on his death in sorrow until the dust
swallowed him.

Astonishing, a nightingale should face such doom
From whose bones no flower will bloom.

[*Joyfully*] But I have some astonishing news for you. It is true
that we are not knowledgeable in the art of summoning
spirits, but tonight Ghulbacheh is the guest of us all. He
has brought with him a canvas screen that tells many
bitter stories. He has removed his heavy tombstone,
risen from the depths of his grave, and come here with
much difficulty. He is now resting, preparing to come
on stage. His minor apprentices will tell you the first
part of the story, and finally Master Gholamhoseyn
Ghulbacheh will tell you the main part of it.

*He exits from the side of the curtain. Drums are heard and the
curtain slowly opens. A huge painted canvas is placed at the
back of the stage. The canvas is fully lit.*

2

The lights gradually dim and the drum beats subside. A spotlight lights up a corner of the backdrop. It is a picture of a city, its houses in ruins, walls crumbled, and a handful of people, old and young, women and children, sit among the rubble. With a beat of a drum, the light goes off, and another corner of the backdrop is lit. It is a big city with tall buildings, large squares, most of the walls fallen down, its population in flight. As the drum beats, the light goes out, lights up another section showing a number of people listening to a speaker. Another section is shown: a large cemetery. Around each grave is a group of people. The light goes out then on, then shows several helicopters in flight. With the beat of a drum, a number of cars are stopped in the middle of a valley and people here and there anxiously look around. With the beat of a drum, lights dim, then brighten to show people sitting in group and individual trenches. Then the lights go off and on, accompanied by the drum. Bodies blown to bits, lacking arms and legs, artillery and tanks wretched, a turned over ambulance, some radio equipment on a hill with a corpse next to it, with a receiver in its hand, and another picture of this kind. The lights come on all at once. The FIRST STORYTELLER stands next to the backdrop with a long staff in his hand and shakes his head.

FIRST STORYTELLER: Oh my, oh my! The great humorist poet had said, "Let me tell you a story true, the meaning of which will befuddle you." Today, we tell you stories that scare the pants off you. Where are you, Master Borzu? [*Master Borzu, the SECOND STORYTELLER enter.*]

SECOND STORYTELLER: Right here, Master Abbas.

FIRST STORYTELLER: What is war?

SECOND STORY-TELLER: War? It's fighting, quarreling, and engaging in battle. We also have the term, warrior, which means brave and courageous. There are other terms, like combatant and fighter, which basically mean the same. War, as an adjective, also refers to tools and equipment and supplies, such as swords, bows and arrows, clubs, maces and mortars, stokers and pokers, planes and bombs, spears and spikes, daggers and knives, canteens...

FIRST STORYTELLER: Everyone knows that.

SECOND STORYTELLER: We also have fake wars, which means pretending to fight someone so other people think there is actually a war.

FIRST STORYTELLER: Will wonders never cease!

He moves to another spot.

SECOND STORYTELLER: But there are different kinds of war. For example, hand-to-hand combat. For example, if you and I get into a fight, we grapple with each other and whoever gets the other's back to the floor is the victor.

FIRST STORYTELLER: That's called wrestling. In hand-to-had combat, the soldiers of the two armies form two lines, and one man from each side enters the battle field, and if one of them is killed, all hell breaks loose and the soldiers begin to fight.

SECOND STORYTELLER: But these days hand-to-hand combat has been set aside. Warmongers sit in their hideaways while the poor people, the unlucky, youths in their prime, become targets for bullets. They don't know that if the warmongers decide to fight, they make the world a hell for their enemies.

FIRST STORYTELLER [*speaks very quickly*]: Let's dispense with family wars, clan wars, wars between two countries, regional wars, and world wars. Tell me, Master, what are the gains of war?

SECOND STORYTELLER: Destruction, hunger, famine, homelessness, death, snakes, rats, and clerics.

FIRST STORYTELLER: Clerics?

SECOND STORYTELLER: Yes, when you give up the ghost, the cleric comes and eats the sweets.

FIRST STORYTELLER and SECOND STORYTELLER [shouting]: Death, rats snakes, clerics. [Silence. They wipe their brows.]

FIRST STORYTELLER: If that's how it is, why do the world's leaders praise war and death so much? Especially religious leaders?

SECOND STORYTELLER: Of course, the leader of the oppressed of the world has said, "Following the teachings of the Prophet is more than prayer and fasting, more than going to the mosque. The main thing is war."

FIRST STORYTELLER: And another time he said, "Praise to those who truly answer God's call by going to war."

SECOND STORYTELLER: He also said, "For death, this youth's bed is small."

FIRST STORYTELLER: Meaning?

SECOND STORYTELLER: Meaning, make him a comfortable grave, so he can rest in peace.

FIRST STORYTELLER: Who is guilty of concupiscence?

SECOND STORYTELLER: He who opposes war.

FIRST STORYTELLER: What is the Great Holy War?

SECOND STORYTELLER: Burnishing the mirror of the heart. And cleansing the soul of impurity.

FIRST STORYTELLER: And what is a minor holy war?

SECOND STORYTELLER: Warring with an enemy and being martyred. That is, as soon as you are killed, the mirror of your heart is burnished.

FIRST STORYTELLER: What if you become a martyr in a war but are captured instead?

SECOND STORYTELLER [calmly and emphatically]: Well, there is a book in English entitled *Captivity from the Islamic Point of View*, and in that book is a statement which baffles all the writers and philosophers in the world, because they have not yet reached this degree of genius and intellectual perfection. It states: "Those who are captured have taken death captive and the captives of Islam are the guests of light."

FIRST STORYTELLER: What do they do to help the combatants and fighters?

SECOND STORYTELLER: Prayers; they perform entreating prayers.

FIRST STORYTELLER: And for the martyrs?

SECOND STORYTELLER: Day of Glorification. On this day, one of the high-ranking religious scholars visits the father of the martyr, has lunch and tea with him, and smokes a water pipe.

FIRST STORYTELLER: And others?

SECOND STORYTELLER: They go to the cemeteries and take gifts to the martyrs.

FIRST STORYTELLER: Gifts for the dead?

SECOND STORYTELLER: Yes, cash donations and war bonds.

FIRST STORYTELLER: What do the dead do with them?

SECOND STORYTELLER: They donate them to the government.

FIRST STORYTELLER: And the government accepts them?

SECOND STORYTELLER: Of course. Haven't you heard the Arabic phrase, "Good comes from the sword"? For instance, the government constantly refers to the spoils of war. It puts greater value on war veteran artists, writers, poets, scholars, and war-stricken cities.

FIRST STORYTELLER: So, war is the gift of God.

SECOND STORYTELLER: Those who do not fight have rejected God's gift.

FIRST STORYTELLER: War, war to victory!

SECOND STORYTELLER: To final victory!

FIRST STORYTELLER: Where is the final victory?

SECOND STORYTELLER: In Karbala, the sacred shrine of Imam Hoseyn in Iraq.

FIRST STORYTELLER: Not Karbala, Jerusalem!

SECOND STORYTELLER: To obtain the sacred sites! In other words, all the sites that the Jews are controlling and the other one which is controlled by the Global Oppressors.

FIRST STORYTELLER: The Association for the Management of the Two Shrines has been established. One cannot sit by silently. The East and the West must be broken thus [*as if breaking a stick of wood on his knee*].

SECOND STORYTELLER: With the mass of those eager for martyrdom in the Fajr Operation.

FIRST STORYTELLER: The Fath Operation.

SECOND STORYTELLER: The Zafar Operation.

FIRST STORYTELLER: The Qa'em al-e Mohammad Operation.

SECOND STORYTELLER: The Nur Operation.

FIRST STORYTELLER: The Meymak Operation.

SECOND STORYTELLER: All good comes from the sword.

FIRST STORYTELLER: What a pity they make so few swords nowadays.

SECOND STORYTELLER: Today's swords are tanks, artillery, machine guns and anti-aircraft guns.   In fact, we also have air swords. F-5s, the Mirage, the Squadron. We also have underground swords, such as "mines" that are buried in the ground.

FIRST STORYTELLER: So, for this religious obligation, it is also necessary to have propaganda?

SECOND STORYTELLER: Yes, it is necessary to have propaganda to take a mystic flight towards the Worshipped One.   The common people, who are like four-legged animals, often do not understand, and for this reason the elders say, Only those who have wealth are afraid of war; those who have nothing are not afraid of war. It is for no reason that they preach in religious gatherings that if people do not understand what martyrdom is, the national economy will be destroyed. Propaganda, yes, gentlemen, it is necessary. We have a Director of War Propaganda. We have a War Week. And every day of the week has a name and a title. For instance, the third day of War Week is Economic Battle Day. That is, it is

obligatory for all Moslems to fast and, on that day, produce more products. The fourth day is the Day of Worship, in other words, the day of Komeyl and Tavassol
prayers. They must recite all the Koranic verses that are
about war. [*Suddenly he assumes a non-theatrical, familiar
tone.*] Ah, I am tired. Take the staff and continue, so I
can rest a bit.   [*Throws the staff to the FIRST
STORYTELLER, who catches it in mid-air.   The FIRST
STORYTELLER, who is holding his forehead, exits and the
lights are turned off.*]

3

The stage is lit.   The FIRST STORYTELLER, in a different costume, stands in front of the curtain, holding his staff.

FIRST STORYTELLER: It has been said and it is said in reliable war chronicles that the land of Dara and the country of Berbers is called Iran, because it must be destroyed [*viran* in Persian]. In old dictionaries, too, it is stated that there is little difference between "i" and "v." We don't have to fuss about "v." The architects of the destruction of Iran were of all sorts and all ilks. For instance, powerful, lofty kings, masters of the word and knowledge, of artillery, with auspicious family trees, strategists and worshippers of war, owners of fast steeds, riders of magnificent chariots, with their stomachs filled with partridges, pheasants, and chickens, inflated with the air of pride, success, and power, with the dagger of injustice strapped to their waists and the sword of justice on their laps, sometimes sitting on an emerald throne, leaning against a bejeweled cushion, burping with their neck veins swollen, resting in an afternoon sleep, constantly thinking [*in a low voice*], which tribe should I kill, whom should I destroy, so that they can refer to me as His Majesty? And whenever they would awaken from sleep, they would get on fast horses, the soldiers ahead and the retinue behind, leap from God's earth with fiery sword in hand, galloping like a meteor, not recognizing friends from foes, and from right flank to left flank killing everyone, and at night, next to a beautiful maiden on a bejeweled pillow, they would not forget war, since as the poet has said:

Go fight in war, do not ask the pleasure,
Because war is an eternal treasure.

The lords and rulers of the provinces, too, who sat in forty-pillar or twenty-pillar palaces, or those only with a few pillars, after extensive burps would shout aloud: "An army is needed; a war is needed; the spoils of war are needed." The most powerful king has sent an emphatic decree that all provinces must be fortified. So, beat and kill everyone, from Esfahan to Shahr-e Rey, from Zabol to Balkh, from Birjand to Baghdad, from Golabdarreh to Jidda, from Maragheh to Shiraz, from Quchan to Ardakan, overthrow everyone, kill everyone, kill the rich, kill the poor. Because anyone who is killed will be rewarded in the next world. Not only did the rulers of the provinces do so, but even the village heads of the most remote small villages did so. The poet has said:

Go to war, war, as joyful as a song,
Life is short, only a few days long.

In support of this blessed matter, the revered religious scholars always spoke about the wisdom of war, the blessings of war, and the gift of war. They would say that he who does not engage in war will be in chains in the depths of Hell forever, and at that time he will have to face the brave warriors. As for peace, according to divine rules, it is the source of misfortune, misery, and abjectness and is Satanic.

A man of God goes to war to fight,
Satan fears war and men of might.

[*Pauses for a moment.*] Now that you understand this matter, then you can also understand why the chief magistrate of the courts has stated that everyone, from the revered leader to the ghetto-dwellers who have no guardians, opposes peace. Peace is shameful, gentlemen. It is the source of disgrace. It is the essence of infamy. On the first day, when God created Adam, He created him for war. Adam, greetings upon him, was fighting alone in the Garden of Eden. He constantly made threats with his clenched fist, and because he had no rival, he threatened himself. [*He imitates Adam with clenched fists in the air, who once in a while punches himself.*] Ouch! it hurts. [*He grabs his rib.*] My rib is broken. [*He writhes from pain on the ground and then gets up.*] Yes, as a result of war, Adam's rib breaks. Well, at that time, there was no bone-setting. Now, what could be done with this broken rib? So God turns that broken rib into Eve. So Adam is no longer suffering from the pain of a broken rib and also loneliness.Because Adam was a brave, belligerent man who sought martyrdom, the first thing he did was to give Eve a good beating. And from that time on, beating women became a religious matter. Eve, too, was a supporter of war. She first gave birth to two sons, Cain and Abel. Yes, such a belligerent woman. They give birth to belligerent men. And what do these two brothers do, gentlemen? Before they can open their eyes, before they can stand on their feet, they charge at each other and start the beating. One of the brothers tears out the liver of the other and then sits by his corpse, sad and confused, because there is no one to kill him. And also, what is he to do with the corpse? Suddenly, he sees a crow burying a walnut in the ground, and so he learns the protocol for burial from the crow and buries his martyred brother in the ground. The burial protocol is also a gift of the High Heavens. The Jews are wrong, who say first was the word, and the word was with God, and God was the word. What kind of nonsense is this? His reverence, Ayatollah Meshkini, the famed war seeker, is writing a book in which he states: First was war, and war was with God, and God was war.

You must go to war, the Almighty has said:
Remove from his shoulders your enemy's head.

When they say, the victory of blood over the sword, what does it mean? Think about it a minute, gentlemen. It means that the sword must spill so much blood and be so stained by blood that it cannot be seen anymore. Understand this point:

For the spilling of blood, use the sword or knife,
Shoot an arrow to put an end to life.

[*He walks to the front of the stage, angrily shouting.*] Now, when your great grand-daddy fought, and all the prophets fought, should you just be sitting by with one hand folded on the other? Why don't you go and become martyrs? Don't you have a grain of honor, bravery? War is a means for bloodletting; it will purify your soul. Any place your blood is spilt on the ground [*sentimentally*], tulips grow. [*Disgustedly*] Not filth, such as violets, hyacinths, clover, celery, eggplant, petunias, lilies, basil, wheat flower, squash, asparagus, and expensive flowers. No, only tulips. Tulips are the sign of blood, the sign of the sword, bayonets, mortar launchers, missile launchers, and especially RPG-7s.

Wherever blood spills, tulips will grow
Peace brings naught but wheat to sow.

It should not be unknown to knowledgeable persons and they should know that the custom of peace, compromise, brotherhood, kindness, and love is in fact abandoning hostility, fighting, belligerency, and quarrel. This heinous custom must be eradicated forever.

Peace breeds naught but calamity;
Eradicate peace, and save humanity.

[*Pause.*] It is true that many high-ranking storytellers possess swords, but we wandering storytellers carry a thin staff instead of a sword. I am boring you and have made myself tired. Where are you, Master Borzu? Take it and continue. [*He throws the staff and Master Borzu, the SECOND STORYTELLER, catches it in the air. The canvas is fully lit.*]

4

The SECOND STORYTELLER looks at the whole canvas in amazement. He points to the upper right corner with the staff.

SECOND STORYTELLER: Where is this place, gentleman? This is the city of Jabalqa. It is abandoned in a dark corner. [*He points to the lower left corner of the canvas.*] What do they call this place? The city of Jabalsa. To hell with both for having taken residence in books but not having yet been competent to find a place on our earthly globe. In between these two cities, there are many countries. Look here. This is a country called Tulipland, with a hundred thousand warriors, all adorned with the tools of battle, including helmets, armors, bayonets, bows and arrows, cannons, shining steel tanks, bejeweled emerald guns, diamond-studded revolvers, and Phantoms jets decorated with strings of agate. And the people, all resemble furious elephants and formidable lions, sitting behind anti-aircraft guns decorated with enamel work, gritting their teeth in anger, with arrows drawn, sitting in ambush, awaiting the mortar fire of the bloodthirsty enemy. [*He takes a few steps back and shows another corner of the canvas.*] And here is a country with blood on its face. All are learned, seekers of knowledge, everywhere refreshing baths and pleasant gardens with flowers and greenery, crystal clear streams flowing everywhere, multi-story houses all built with the plaster, limestone, cement, and concrete of knowledge and philosophy, and decorated with dignity, wisdom and literature. This city with a bloody face has only one powerful warrior, awesome, like a fighting cock, one eyebrow higher and another lower, his mustache reaching his ears, calling out for challengers, whose name is the Lion-Catching, Tiger-Killing, Cobra-Eating Babraz Khan. He is so terrifying that even such legendary champions as Sam, son of

Nariman, and Rostam would tremble like a willow tree
if they came face to face with him. He always knows
that he is victorious and the enemy defeated. He does
not believe in anything but the strength of his arms and
his own might. He constantly eats and drinks and beats
his chest saying, "Victory is ours, defeat belongs to you,"
pointing to the country of Tulipland. In comparing the
balance of power between these two countries, he said:
"One warrior is better than a hundred thousand others."
Now hear about the fact that warriors cannot sit idly by.

One day, in a drunken stupor, the famed Babraz Khan
sets off the cannon. Suddenly, a huge cannonball as
large as the Damavand Peak, no, even the size of Saran-
dib Mountain, fell on Tulipland. The warriors of Tulipland, who were all taking their afternoon nap, rose up
in confusion, put their helmets on, prepared the guns
and mortar launchers, and in the blink of an eye, shouting and cursing, leveled the country of blood-face, like
the thundering roar of a volcano. They destroyed the
baths and crushed the flower and fruit gardens, turned
the streams into dry ditches, and eradicated knowledge
and philosophy from cement and concrete. They made
mothers mourn their offspring. It reached a point that
high-level positions appeared. People constantly gathered the dead, washed them, and ditched them with or
without burial shrouds in the ground of misery. But the
Cobra-Eating Babraz Khan, who did not believe in
submission, cried out and called to his sleeping friends.
All the aged ancient Babraz Khans poured out of the
caves, greased the ancient arsenals, and engaged in the
sacred practice of war. Each side began to strike, and
such a war ignited between Tulipland and the Blood-
Faced Country that the denizens of both lands began to
scream and shout, and the sages of both countries composed a similar verse on the same day, at the same hour
and second, which people began to recite:

Soon we will all be eradicated,
Glass broken, wine spilled, and the cup-bearer elimi-
nated.

Of course, the wine and cup-bearer were only the result of delicate and poetic minds, but in fact all the glass was broken and scattered, cities were destroyed and houses demolished. The fate of the people of these two countries reached a point that both learned dancing and began dancing all the time. Why? Because ground-to-ground missiles were launched from both sides and people had to jump up for the missiles to pass under them. Look at this corner and that corner. Look here, gentlemen. Everyone is dancing. They jump up and down to elude the missiles, mortars, and RPG-7s. Yes, dancing began from that time. If there had been no war, there would be no dancing. If war is the gift of God, dancing is also the gift of God. It is obligatory for everyone to fight or to dance. This humble servant has composed the following lines on this subject:

Two old companions are war and dance
For dancing to appear, war must advance.
Put one hand on the waist, the other on the trigger,
And the number of dead becomes bigger and bigger.
The grave is no more than an eiderdown bed
And the one who knows it is the one who is dead.

[*Pauses and then places his hand under his chin and squatting looks at the audience.*] Oh my, I talked too much and my chin got tired. A chin is a chin; it is not a machine gun. Oh, dear benefactors, I had better pass this thick staff to the master to see what he has to say. [*He throws the staff. The FIRST STORYTELLER catches it in mid-air in the middle of the stage. The SECOND STORYTELLER exits, dead tired.*]

5

FIRST STORYTELLER: I'm about to gag on Master Borzu's long-windedness. I don't want to be rude. I'm the lowliest of his students. I shall be painlessly brief. Narrators and storytellers, the masters of wit and lords of speech, must speak little and selectively. But these days, the world has changed. Hearts are aching. Everyone has been enslaved.

I am ashamed, this life to endure,
to be a master, yet be a slave.
To fear true words, I do assure,
is worse than not knowing the King from a knave.

Yes, one mustn't be afraid. One must open one's heart and say what needs to be said. Enough elocution. [*His mood changes. Quickly and nimbly he stands at the foot of the backdrop and points to a section.*] Look here, gentlemen. This part. A man has fled a bombing. As he was fleeing, he picked up his child in an alley and put it under his arm. He jumped into an airplane and went to a ruined village and maybe had a little sip of water. Now, look over here, gentlemen. He sees that the child isn't his. What? Instead of his own offspring, he has picked up another child and fled. When he tries to give the child water, he sees the child doesn't understand a word he is saying. He is Armenian, gentlemen. Now, look over here at this section. An Armenian woman has picked up the man's child and is giving it water in another village when she suddenly realizes the child isn't hers. What is that called? The glory of war? In war, everything is jumbled up. Everything is switched. Another child in place of yours sits on your lap and looks at you strangely, afraid of the war and afraid of strangers. You don't understand it and it doesn't understand you.

[Quickly] Now, look here and listen well, gentlemen. *[Indicates another section]* This is a small village inhabited by a handful of poor villagers. And now look over here. *[Indicates another section]* Here is the country's capital. There are buildings and houses. What streets and squares and promenades! It has everything, gentlemen. Here live nobles and aristocrats, people of good family, the wealthy with good names, grandees of majesty, pomp and grandeur. They live with peace of mind, to some extent. Because this is the capital, a prince's horse cannot be called a nag. Look, gentlemen, some planes come suddenly and drop bombs. *[Sound of bombs, screaming and shouting, weeping and wailing, falling rubble.]* Then what happens? All the nobles, aristocrats, and dignitaries jump from their sweet sleep, hold onto their pant strings, and escape. *[Sound of pleading, shouting, cries for help, swearing and cursing.]* They can't get their cars out of the parking lots. There are no safe places. They get on a dilapidated truck, one for hauling bricks. The truck now carries the gentlemen instead of bricks. All of them are hungry, thirsty, and frightened. They arrive at a village. *[Shows the small village]* The truck dumps the gentlemen. Of their pomp, majesty, and grandeur, nothing remains. *[In the tone of a eulogist and mourner]* All that they have left is fear and terror. They are hungry! They are thirsty! They are empty-handed, with blistered feet. From the blessed shower of bombs, pride and arrogance have fled from their jowls. They only fear for their lives. The poor inhabitants of the village sit among the rubble smoking water pipes. The gentlemen worry about what to do. Money? What is money? They have nothing left. They don't laugh and strut, swagger, and parade anymore. The souvenir they have brought is only the blessed word: escape. At night they are content with dry bread, old yogurt, and fetid water. Oh, gentlemen! *[seriously]* But the next day do you know what happens? *[very seriously]* The villagers, or as sociologists or socio-logues say, the rural dwellers, put them to work. Haj Samsamossalaneh picks beets. His Honor Salalatossadat digs up potatoes. Haj Aqa

Kamal Qomashchi takes the sheep out to graze. Meanwhile, the villagers sit on a hill and smoke pipes and prattle and laugh at the gentlemen's groomed beards. At sunset, when everyone comes from their work, [*emphatically*] the villagers throw the gentlemen some water and yogurt and bread, then give them a place in ruined stables. [*Suddenly begins to laugh and covers his mouth with his hand.*] Sometimes strange things happen. Look here, gentlemen. Sometimes these villagers ride the gentlemen piggyback. At sunset, they get on the shoulders of the great ones and ride them around a square. What a cruel world. "Sometimes you ride in the saddle, sometimes the saddle rides on you." [*singing*]

From prosperous Tehran, a singular man fleeing said
   with a sigh and in sadness,
Woe be unto the merciless plan which suddenly shat
   tered our every gladness.
When bombs fell, there were two or three, down upon us
   from the sky,
They crashed down, upon you and me, smashing our
   world into bits, by and by.
Once all our tables were filled to the brim with food that
   for others was a loss.
Now we are servants of beggars, so grim, and fill our bel
   lies with garbage they toss.
Spit on you, oh war, spit on you for making swans of the
   miserable crow.

But the swan has not fought the war of the crow. War has stricken everyone. Calamity has descended upon the heads of ravens and cravens, crows and pros. [*STORYTELLER MASTER BORZU jumps in the middle of the stage and takes the staff from him. STORYTELLER ABBAS sits in a corner, hugs his knees, and lights a cigarette.*]

6

SECOND STORYTELLER: For instance, [*points to one corner*]
what do you see here? If you don't understand, I'll explain it to you. Here is a gentleman, a real gentleman.
Look at his face; check out his looks. See his frown!
Look at the way he smokes a cigarette, gentlemen. See,
gentlemen, he is wearing a torn undershirt, full of holes,
like a colander. It's as if he has been the target of a machine gun. And whee, what a pretty tie he is wearing,
sitting on a platform; on one foot, he has a blue slipper
and on the other a brown one. He is deep in thought
and contemplation. Sometimes he laughs and sometimes he cries. He does not want to show any weakness.
He talks incessantly; he talks to himself; he talks to his
relatives and to those close to him. Listen!

The stage is semi-dark. The MAN's face is brightly lit.

VOICE OF THE MAN: I studied al-Abdan for a lifetime. I ran
and ran and did not get anywhere. I studied theology
and talked and talked, but said nothing. In the end, I
had to get somewhere. I would have to make a better
world. I ran and ran and reached the Azari Intersection.
I set out into the alleys and back alleys, and when I
opened my eyes I saw, oh my, a group of people wandering around everywhere without any guardian. I decided to establish a regular sufficient subsistence for the
people, which I did, and regular subsistence was established for all of us. And suddenly, what did I become? I
became a gentleman, Mr. Mouse. [*Laughing for no reason*]
I went and went and bought myself a book on anti-
dourine and kept reading it. And I kept looking for
dourine itself, which I could not find. There were other
things, too, I don't remember. Have you heard the story
of Mr. Crow, who was sitting on a tree eating yogurt?

And I saw a woman's shoe, which was made of live snakes. Then I went and went until I reached a large square full of small and big children, all pale and yellow and chubby, with and without moustaches, who were playing volleyball and football with several pretty cannonballs. I asked them to light my cigarette. They lit my cigarette with a bomb. I came and sat on this platform. Now my cigarette is about to finish. Do you have any cigarettes, to give me a few? Do you have a bomb to light my cigarette? I like smoking cigarettes like this. I also like halva, sweetmeats, and sugar rations. If you don't have cigarettes, give me a pair of handwoven cotton slippers. I am disabled, tired. I don't want anything. Give me a cigarette and light my cigarette with a bomb. If you have it, if you don't have it. [*The VOICE slowly fades, along with the light.*] If you have it, if you don't, a cigarette...a bomb...

SECOND STORYTELLER: Do you know what has happened to him? He has lost his mind. But wind in his hand has been added to his misfortune. He begs for bombs to light his cigarettes. He who has a fist full of dust in his palm has a fistful of dust. But wind in the hand means being drowned in the ocean of destitution. It means losing the mind and running aimlessly in the desert of madness, like a wandering salamander. [*He shows a corner of the canvas.*] Where is this? The front. What is the front? The forehead? No, gentlemen, it is the front of the war. Look at this young man, who is a revolutionary guard, who has lost his life and is on the ground. And this is another brother guard. They have gone to war to do what? To fight alongside other guards. Against whom? Against the other side, behind the canvas, whom you do not see. The line of the enemy, all angry:

Two armies of brave ability
Align to fight with hostility.

Artillery fire from this side and that. Machine gun fire from this side and that. From morning to late at night, constantly this exchange continues and:

Black and dark turned the day, like the night
The sun disappeared and hid from sight.

At night, one of the guard brothers thinks about worship and prayers. He decides to perform his prayers first, not the obligatory prayers, but the evening prayers for the lonely away from home. Since it has been said:

I begin the evening prayers, crying
Telling stories in loneliness, sighing
Remembering homeland and friends, I mourn
Longing never from home again to be torn.

Yes, this dull-brained young man fills his ewer with water in the trench and starts up the hill to wash up. He does not heed the warning of others. First he engages in an act of nature, and at that exact moment when he picks up the ewer to wash himself in the front and back, [*in a strong tone*] an enemy mortar lands and cuts off his arm from the shoulder. The hand holding the ewer ascends towards heaven to meet with God. Suddenly, it falls on the flying carpet of the Prophet Solomon, which was passing by. The hand turns the ewer to wash the buttocks, but alas there is no buttocks, gentlemen. The ewer strives to pour some water, but there is no hand to help it. Now, hear of the fellow fighters of this brother in the trench, who climb the hill to remove this shattered flower. But the mortar does not give them respite. In a few seconds, the Prophet Solomon's carpet is filled with shredded buttocks, and the hard-working hand of their old friend finds the ewer and begins to...

FIRST STORYTELLER, MASTER ABBAS [*takes the stick forcefully from BORZU. They both look at each other in anger. MASTER ABBAS bites his lip. Another corner of the canvas is lit.*] Here stands a twig of a kid and next to him another twig of a kid. Both are revolutionaries. Both are followers of the ideology. There is not just one or two of them, there are many—the unripe plums of the Islamic revolution. These poor things have swarmed every-where, like roaches.

He is silent. The sound of a group of kids singing an anthem.

VOICES [*run together*]: Did you steel my pencil? When is your brother going to be martyred? I want almonds. My fa-ther said last night, if things continue this way, I've got to get Ahmad out of the country somehow. Do you think an Uzi is better or a G-3? Why doesn't the beet seller come by the school anymore? Does your mother pray? A smuggler is supposed to bring a chicken to our house. Could you guess what's in this backpack? I found it in our alley. [*All these voices are intertwined.*]

FIRST STORYTELLER: These youths of the revolution all intend to go to the front of the War of Truth Against Falsehood, to make the tulip garden of the martyrs more colorful with their own blood. But the enemies of the revolution, or rather counterrevolutionaries, that is, the parents of these self-sacrificers of the revolution, oppose their going to the front. Look here. [*Points to a corner.*] This is by the entrance of Sajjad Mosque, that is, the mosque of the Infirm Holy Imam. What do you see? The same first two twigs of kids. They have come to report to the offi-cials that their parents support peace. Look carefully, look at this corner. The parents have been arrested. They are standing by the wall with blinders on. The revolutionaries, their children, are shooting the support-ers of peace and the enemies of war. [*Sound of a firing squad. The STORYTELLER in an epic tone.*]

You who are hesitant to kill your foe
May not be called a revolutionary, you know.
If you have killed your son and your mother
To secure the world from the hostile other,
Or you have killed the opponents of war

You shall reside in Paradise forevermore.

Now, where are these parents? In the freezing pits of hell. And those two war-seeking children, by the Tree of Tuba or the Kowsar Pond in Paradise. The fate of the storekeepers who sell for cash or credit is happier than that of the war-seekers and seekers of peace. [*Throws the staff to the other STORYTELLER.*]

SECOND STORYTELLER, BORZU [*sarcastically*]: Do you know what is left of war? It is not only paradise. Sometimes it is a raspberry. It is not always guns. Sometimes it is broken junk. [*In the tone of a professional mourner*] Sometimes it is an old shoe, sometimes a broken sword, sometimes a disabled armored tank, and sometimes a man in armor who has fallen on the ground. The first is made of steel, and the second is a human being. The first has its lid blown up, in one corner is an empty beer can and in another corner kitchen utensils used behind the front. In one corner there is a field telephone and in another corner the pipe of an antiaircraft gun. Trenches all side-by-side. Trenches for a single person and for double occupancy. Trenches for five or more people. Everywhere empty canteens and on the top of the hills shredded flags. At the foot of a hill, the carcass of a mule with empty barrels. And everywhere full of bloody corpses. On every corner, a socket with an eye popped out that has no eyelids, but blinks, looking for the eyes. But instead of the eye, the tongue of a scrawny dog enters the socket and licks the hole that is filled with coagulated blood in order to survive. At the foot of the hill is a hand, which feels around, looking for a weapon, to pull the trigger. Ears scattered everywhere, looking for fingers to block the sounds of war. There are also many legs, which want to run away but have lost their owners. Everywhere, large numbers of hearts, entrails, stomachs, and intestines are scattered around.

Yes, gentlemen, look! Due to the benefits of war, the soldier, the self-sacrificer, and the martyr, before joining

God, are holding a bowl of water from the Kowsar Pond in Paradise and, in fact, are drinking the "sherbet of martyrdom." Where did this bowl come from? And where did the sherbet come from? From Paradise? You are mistaken, this bowl of water has come from the bottom of a well. Who has brought this sherbet of martyrdom? The Imam of the Age! From where? From the bottom of the well. Because of the War of Truth Against Falsehood, the Imam of the Age has returned before his time. Don't you believe me? Look at this corner, gentlemen. His Holiness the Twelfth Imam has appeared in a white garb on a white horse and like a water carrier hands the combatants the sherbet of martyrdom. There are not just one or two combatants. Some have fallen to the ground just at the border. The Imam of the Age goes to the other side of the border by mistake to give them the sherbet of martyrdom, and the enemies suddenly see a rider in white on a white horse entering their territory.

First, they think it is a trick and want to eliminate the Imam with a mortar. But in the manner of generals, they look through binoculars and advance with hesitation, because they think that the ancient war trick is underway. Warriors always know about war tricks and think it is the Trojan War and many warriors are hiding in the belly of the horse, armed with all sorts of weapons. They come closer slowly and see that the horse is so thin that its ribs are showing, as if the rider is sitting on a skeleton of a horse. [*The STORYTELLER bursts out in loud laughter.*] But you don't know the rest of the story. [*He gets up.*] Look here, gentlemen. The enemies capture the Imam of the Age and take him to the military base. The Imam of the Age is trembling with fear. They place a pail of water before his horse and hand him a bowl of water. Before the Imam of the Age can take a sip, still trembling, they ask him: Who are you? The Imam of the Age does not say anything, and the enemy wants to make him confess. Then they light a cigarette and give it to the Imam of the Age. The Imam of the Age takes a couple of puffs and regains his composure somewhat. But he cannot say anything. The enemy asks him again:

Who are you? He answers: I am the Imam of the Age.
The enemy all burst out laughing. No one can imagine
such a scrawny sickly-looking Imam of the Age. Then
one of the enemies draws his .45-caliber colt from his
hip, steps forward, and places it at the temple of the
Imam of the Age. The Imam of the Age says: Please
have mercy; my mother is waiting for me. Then he sees
several people approaching him with weapons. Fearing
for his life, gentlemen, the Imam of the Age begins to
confess. You know what he says? Let the Imam say it
himself. [*Two IRAQI SOLDIERS throw the IMAM, with
hands tied, on the stage.*]

IMAM OF THE AGE: I swear I am a freshman student in dramatic arts, and in order to provide for my blind father
and disabled mother, I had to join the Revolutionary
Guard Corps, and because I was not capable of combat
and did not know anything about war operations, I was
employed in the Dramatic Division of the Guard Corps
and played the role of the Imam of the Age.

SECOND STORYTELLER, MASTER BORZU [*laughing*]:   The
enemy asks the Imam of the Age:

FIRST IRAQI SOLDIER: Are there any other Imams of the Age
than you?

IMAM OF THE AGE: Many in Aliabad, near Qom. When the
Amal Group established its main base there, in addition
to training guards and combatants of Islam, they also
trained artists and actors to...

SECOND IRAQI SOLDIER: How many of you were there?

IMAM OF THE AGE: Well, 124 persons.

SECOND STORYTELLER, MASTER BORZU: For the love of
God, give me a glass, too, I am very thirsty. [*Pauses*]
Now, if you don't give it to me, at least give it to all these
people who are here... In any case... But look here, gen-

tlemen. [*He kicks the IMAM OF THE AGE and the IRAQI SOLDIERS.*] Get lost! Let us get back to our business.

The SOLDIERS and the IMAM OF THE AGE exit.

Is it enough or should I say more? No, we are all tired. Let us catch our breath until it is time for Master Gholamhoseyn Ghulbacheh to tell you the main story.

INTERMISSION

7

Before the curtain opens, we hear the sound of several horrendous explosions, breaking glass, men and women screaming and shouting, children crying, people fleeing and, continually, frightened cries. When the curtain opens we see bricks and stones, large and small, mixed up together. There are personal belongings and broken dishes, bodies blown to bits, human hands and feet, bloody heads strewn this way and that. The STORYTELLER, BORZU, who was caught in the rubble, pulls himself out and flees. The sounds of explosions and moans reach our ears from afar; they subside slowly. GHOLAMHOSEYN GHULBACHEH enters. He holds the STORYTELLER's staff. He goes to the debris and looks at it, walks around looking at the mutilated bodies. Depressed and frowning, he squats down. The original canvas has been changed. In addition to various views, there are several large animated faces with agitated expressions. They are blinking, weeping, burping, worrying, occasionally nodding off. Suddenly one of the faces sneezes, and Ghulbacheh gets up.

GHULBACHEH: It's an old saying that all things come to those who wait. But I say, he who hesitates is lost. If you wait and are patient, nothing will go your way. What you'll get is degradation and misery. Waiting and sitting on your hands just makes things worse. The more you wait and bite your tongue and stay still, the more you can be sure you're done for. If you understand this, we'll go back to the main story. Yes, you saw what you saw. I'm not disputing it. But my story is another story. For a lifetime, I told the story of Sohrab's death to everyone, and my cold words had no effect on anyone's warm heart. Without recourse, I closed the book of life and was laid to rest in my grave. Tonight they dragged me here by force. I may be the first person to have come from the grave before the Seraph blows his horn and mankind gathers on the Desert of Resurrection and appeared on stage. Well, look over there. [*A corner of the canvas is lit.*] Here's a town in the north of Iran. People of every stripe live in this town. I'll tell you the story of only one family. The father is a merchant in the bazaar, who gets by and is respected. The mother is a housewife, always in poor health. These two have a sixteen-year-old son named Jamal. [*As he mentions the FATHER, MOTHER, and JAMAL, their faces are lit up.*] Jamal is being drafted into the war. There is a quarrel in the family. See for yourselves! [*The stage lights dim and when they come back up, GULBACHEH has left the stage and JAMAL'S FATHER and MOTHER have come on.*]

JAMAL'S FATHER [*to JAMAL*]: What are we going to do?

JAMAL: It's obvious what you should do.

JAMAL'S FATHER: I mean, what you should do.

JAMAL: Well, I'm not going to the front.

JAMAL'S MOTHER [*to the FATHER, exasperated*]: Haji, this boy is all we have. Have mercy. Don't let them use him as cannon fodder.

JAMAL'S FATHER: What am I supposed to tell the *komiteh*? What am I supposed to tell the Guard Corps?

JAMAL'S MOTHER: Tell them he's out of town; we don't know where he is.

JAMAL'S FATHER: You think they're stupid? They know everything. They know what you do in the back closet of your house in the dark. Do you think they don't know Jamal's in town?

JAMAL: I'll disguise myself and leave tonight.

JAMAL'S FATHER: Where will you go?

JAMAL: I'll go to the mountains.

JAMAL'S FATHER [*angry*]:   So you're just going to change clothes and leave?   What a joke.   Sixteen years I've knocked myself out for you, and now you disgrace me.   I won't be able to hold my head up in public.

JAMAL: You'll manage.   Don't worry.   It won't cost you anything.

JAMAL'S FATHER: Hell!   They'll close my shop and confiscate everything I own, even our house.   They might even take me off to prison.   Do you know what prison means?

JAMAL: Do you know what the front means?

JAMAL'S FATHER: Yes, I do.   At the front you can breathe free and easy.   But in prison, what would an old man like me do?

JAMAL'S MOTHER [*exasperated*]:   Haji, they're not going to arrest you.   I swear by the Prophet's daughter, they won't bother you.   Maybe they'll wring some money out of you or close your shop, but what's more important, those things or keeping Jamal alive?

JAMAL'S FATHER: Alive?

JAMAL'S MOTHER: He should go get killed?

JAMAL'S FATHER [*calmly, trying to reason with them*]:   Not everybody in a war gets killed.

JAMAL: But I don't know anything about war.

JAMAL'S FATHER: You don't need to.   In one or two weeks, you'll learn shooting, firing, all that stuff.   Other boys weren't born knowing how to do these things.   Don't be afraid, son, nothing will happen.   What you're supposed to do is obvious.   You kill the enemy.   But let's say you get shot in the hand or foot. You bleed two or three little drops, and it hurts a little bit, like being stung by a bee. But there's mercurochrome and dressings and everything. Don't be afraid. Why don't you go right now and present yourself and settle the matter? Well, are you going to go or not?

JAMAL: No!

JAMAL'S FATHER: I swear to God, I'm going to cut you out of my will.

JAMAL: I don't want to be in your will, and I'm not going.

JAMAL'S FATHER [attacks JAMAL, punching and kicking him]: What the hell am I supposed to do with you?

JAMAL'S MOTHER [weeping, tries to separate the two]: Don't hit him, man. Shame on you. You're killing my child!

JAMAL'S FATHER [panting, moves away and wipes the sweat from his forehead. To the MOTHER]: You see what you've raised? The smart aleck stands there and tells his father "no" right to his face. [To JAMAL] I'm sorry for every bite of bread I've ever given you. [Looks at his watch.] I'm late, I have to go to the bazaar and kill myself so you two can feed your faces. [Exits. JAMAL and his MOTHER watch him leave.]

JAMAL'S MOTHER: Don't worry, they'll take you away over my dead body. Come on. I'll tell you what we'll do. [They exit.]

ೞೞ

The stage light is on. GHULBACHEH is on stage and the faces of JAMAL'S FATHER and MOTHER are on the canvas. In place of JAMAL's face is the face of a CLERIC, who has a hideous smile on his lips. From time to time, he also scowls and frowns.

GHULBACHEH: Jamal and his mother devise an escape plan. On his way to his shop, Jamal's father hesitates at a fork in the road. He changes directions and goes to the *komiteh* and to the clergyman who heads it.

FACE OF THE FATHER: Good day, Your Reverence.

FACE OF THE CLERIC [*scowls*]: Good day to you. That no-good boy of yours has never presented himself to us.

FACE OF THE FATHER: He's just come back from a trip out of town. He's at home now. Please send a few Guards to get him.

FACE OF THE CLERIC: Bless you, Haji. God will reward you in the next world.

GHULBACHEH: The Guards charge into the house. They arrest the sixteen-year-old Jamal, who was fleeing over the rooftops, and send him off to the war front. Jamal gradually gives in. He has no choice. Out of desperation, he gets to know one of the other boys, named Esma'il, who is the same age as he. Where is Esma'il from? Look over here. [*A light is shone on a town.*] This is the city known as Esfahan, "half the world," as the saying goes. Everywhere, there are domes and palaces and squares. The Jewel of Persia, like a precious stone shining on the face of the earth. And look here. Here is Esma'il's family's house, and this is his father. [*A FACE is lit; it is crying.*] And this is Esma'il's mother. [*Another FACE is lit.*] And this is Esma'il himself. [*ESMA'IL's face is lit. His brow is knit, and newly-sprouted down covers his face. ESMA'IL and his FATHER and MOTHER are on stage.*]

ESMA'IL'S FATHER [*to ESMA'IL*]: Look, Esma'il, my son, do you know what you're doing?

ESMA'IL: Yes, I know. I want to perform my religious duty.

ESMA'IL'S MOTHER: But you never stop praying and fasting, you go to the mosque, you haven't broken any religious laws.

ESMA'IL: I'm going so I can be a martyr. The Prophet said that those things are not enough; you have to fight for Islam.

ESMA'IL'S FATHER: Do you want to kill your mother and me?

ESMA'IL [*proudly*]: What do you mean, kill you? You should be proud of me. In a country on the wings of God's angels, the real leader of the war is the Hidden Imam. One must surely become a martyr.

ESMA'IL'S FATHER: Look, I have a thousand hopes and dreams for you. I wanted to arrange a respectable job for you and...

ESMA'IL: My occupation is war, fighting. I will take vengeance on the enemy, so that there will be no trace of them left.

ESMA'IL'S FATHER: No trace of whom?

ESMA'IL: The Infidels. Our revolution must spread across the world and the flag of Islam be raised everywhere. His Reverence himself said so from the pulpit. [*As he begins to leave, his parents cling to him, weeping. He kicks and punches them.*] Let me go, or I'll tell the *komiteh*.

ESMA'IL'S FATHER: Stay a little while longer, just one minute. [*ESMA'IL exits.*]

ESMA'IL'S VOICE: I'll write to you and send you my will from the battle lines between good and evil. [*The stage darkens. We hear the sound of women weeping and shrieking and beating their heads and chests.*]

03 80

A MAN'S VOICE: It's alright. God willing, he'll come back safe and sound. Don't make such a racket. They'll show up soon. [*The light on ESMA'IL'S FATHER'S FACE is lit.*]

ESMA'IL'S FATHER'S FACE: I don't know whether he's dead or alive. It's been months and we haven't heard from him. Between my own pain and sorrow and the weeping and wailing of his mother and aunt and the other women, I can't eat a bite or sleep a wink. [*The sound of wailing rises. He shouts.*] Enough already. Shut up! I can't bear the pain of my child being far away, or your crying and screaming. [*Shouts*] Stop it! [*Complete silence. The light on the canvas dims. GHULBACHEH is on stage.*]

GHULBACHEH [*smiling*]: Then one day, after months of waiting and watching the street, a letter for Jamal's father arrives. In it, Jamal says that he is fine and tells of his wonderful life at the front.

JAMAL'S VOICE: Dear Father and Mother, my situation here is very good; there's no need to worry about me at all. They give us water and bread here and sometimes even sweets, though of course they aren't very sweet. We have very good trenches, so if shells don't come in and there are no bombing raids, we can nap for a few hours. I have made a very good friend, named Esma'il. Any time I get fed up with things, he makes me laugh with his Esfahani accent. Any time there's a burst of fire and some guys in the next trench get torn apart and thrown into the air, Esma'il claps his hands and says happily, "You see, it didn't fall on our heads." We are pious and true. Any time a bomb comes toward us, the Imam hits it aside, like a ball, because they aren't pious and true. Thank you, Father, for guiding me down the right path.

All the time the light shines on the faces of JAMAL'S MOTHER and FATHER, who are very happy. The FATHER'S head appears from a hole in the curtain. He tells the MOTHER:

JAMAL'S FATHER: See what I made of that mouse? He's a lion now.

JAMAL'S MOTHER: I hope he comes back OK.

JAMAL'S FATHER: Of course he will. And when he does, I'm going to do everything possible for him.

JAMAL'S MOTHER: What, for example?

JAMAL'S FATHER: First, I'll find him a wife, and we'll have a wedding party that lasts for a week.

The light on the faces of JAMAL'S MOTHER and FATHER are dimmed and the light on ESMA'IL's FATHER's and MOTHER's faces are lit. Both are smiling and happy, as they listen, peeking out, and laugh together.

ESMA'IL'S VOICE: Dear Mother and Father, you can see what miracles faith performs. My situation at the front is excellent. Every day, morning, noon, and night, they give us kabob and rice in the trenches. We have milk and coke and hamburgers. We have nice, warm blankets, mattresses, and pillows that we set out in the bottom of the trenches. We sleep till we're rested and then get up and take a few shots at the enemy. They lose, and we go back to our trenches and eat our kabob and rice and hamburgers and potato stew and eggplant stew and Coke and Canada Dry, and then we sit around and crack nuts. I have made a good friend who is from the north. He's like me, he loves martyrdom very much, and he's so brave that when a trench next to us gets hit and some guys fly into the air, he gets up and shouts, "It's not fair. Why don't they drop one on us? Why are we still denied the gift and blessing of martyrdom?" At every prayer time, he prays, "Oh God, please send a shell burrowing into my chest." But it seems that His Holiness the Hidden Imam is our guardian. My biggest regret is that my tour of duty is almost over, and I'll have to go back soon without getting my wish. Give my regards to everyone in the family, and especially to the prayer leader at the mosque. [*His FATHER and MOTHER laugh with joy, and we hear the laughter of a group of women.*]

ESMA'IL'S FATHER: When he comes back, I'm going to get him a wife and throw a party you'll be able to hear in every corner of this province.

The stage darkens and when it is relit, the CLERIC and JAMAL'S FATHER are seated facing each other.

JAMAL'S FATHER: Your Reverence, I would like to presume to make a major request of Your Excellency.

CLERIC: Please, go ahead.

JAMAL'S FATHER: I wanted to obtain your approval, when Jamal comes back from the front, to come with his mother to visit you and ask for Your Excellency's daughter's hand in marriage to Jamal. You yourself once said from the pulpit that the children of a believing couple will be chaste, self-sacrificing, and pious.

CLERIC: That is correct. But to a large extent, it is a matter of divine will. I personally would have no objection. Many young religious scholars have been recommended, but most preferable would be someone back from the front.

JAMAL'S FATHER: It only shows how generous and self-sacrificing men of the cloth are.

CLERIC: And you must keep in mind that the girl in question, like the daughters of all religious scholars, has no trousseau.

JAMAL'S FATHER: Your Reverence, I am fully aware of this. Of course, such has been the case since old times.

CLERIC: But in the current revolutionary circumstances, some important points must be kept in mind, and those are that an adequate dower must be paid, and a sum to the parents, too, for raising the girl, particularly with regard to the daughters of religious scholars, and especially the children of the descendants of the Prophet.

JAMAL'S FATHER: Yes, of course, that is true. You can rest assured. [*Tambourines and ululation from women are heard from behind the canvas.*]

CLERIC: But there is one other matter. Instruments of joy must not be used in this wedding. Only the banging of tubs or beating of kettledrums will be allowed.

JAMAL'S FATHER: Everything will be carried out according to your instructions. [*Smiles*] And Your Reverence, would it be possible for you to have the *komiteh* deliver a few bags of sugar to my shop? I have taken a vow, and I want to do something for the poor and oppressed.

CLERIC: Actually, I have some business there. Why don't you come along?   [*They get up and the CLERIC follows JAMAL'S FATHER off stage.*]

GHULBACHEH [*snickers*]: Ah, what happy days! Things begin cooking quickly. Everyone, whether in a trench or not, is happy. They are going to have a wedding and funeral ceremonies at the same time, eat cakes for the wedding and halva for the burial, at home and in the cemetery. Anyway, Ghulbacheh mustn't mourn. A mirror-polisher must polish the mirror so everything can be seen clearly. Look. [*The faces of ESMA'IL'S FATHER and MOTHER are lit.*]

ESMA'IL'S FATHER [*sticks his face out of the canvas and addresses ESMA'IL'S MOTHER.*] We should go and ask for the hand of the E'temadzadeh's girl. She's young, pretty, educated, with a respected father, money and land, a good name and a good reputation.

ESMA'IL'S MOTHER: Esma'il will never approve. He'll find a thousand things wrong with her.

ESMA'IL'S FATHER: Like what?

ESMA'IL'S MOTHER: She used to go to school without a veil.

ESMA'IL'S FATHER: That was before the revolution. What does that have to do with now?

ESMA'IL'S MOTHER: She was seen recently in the street with her cousin.

ESMA'IL'S FATHER: Why do you talk about people's children behind their backs?

ESMA'IL'S MOTHER: I swear to you, Esma'il himself once told me that.

ESMA'IL'S FATHER: What about the Eftekhari girl?

ESMA'IL'S MOTHER: No.

ESMA'IL'S FATHER: The Najmabadi girl?

ESMA'IL'S MOTHER: Don't even mention her. She used to work in a hospital.

ESMA'IL'S FATHER: So, who are we going to try?

ESMA'IL'S MOTHER: I know of three girls that he might approve of: Haj Sheikh Ahmad Musavi's girl, Haj Molla Borazjani's girl, and the third one is the sister of Abbas Aqa Meydandar, who's the head of Komiteh III.

ESMA'IL'S FATHER: What strange times we live in. Everything is in their hands, and still they want to pass off their old-maid daughters. I don't know. You choose. Just try to keep our son's future in mind. [*Sounds of tambourines and beating of tubs. A spotlight shines on GHULBACHEH.*]

GHULBACHEH: In all this confusion, a letter from Jamal to his
    father arrives.

JAMAL'S VOICE: My tour of duty is over, and I will be coming
    back in ten days.

GHULBACHEH: The celebrating and rejoicing and happiness
    begin. Frowns disappear and everyone thanks God eve-
    rything has turned out OK. Jamal's father does things
    up in the best possible way. Day and night he loads his
    table with every possible kind of rice, even bejeweled
    rice, whey pottage and yogurt soup, meatballs, cutlets,
    sugar-coated nuts, rock candy, and so forth. And look
    over there! He sits lounging at the head of the table,
    constantly stuffing his face. And every time he drinks
    from his glass, he says, "A curse on Yazid!" During one
    of these celebrations, a letter from Komiteh III arrives,
    and guess what's in it? Good news. "Your son will ar-
    rive tomorrow by helicopter." [*Firmly*] There is an ex-
    plosion of happiness in the house, in the neighbors'
    houses, in the district, in the whole town. [*In a normal
    tone of voice*] From that time on, they are thinking about
    wedding plans. Jamal's mother brings things out of her
    old truck, old cloths, moth-eaten shawls, fine china, al-
    ways thinking of everything she has left to do.

MIXED WOMEN'S VOICES:

> Let's make sweet rice.
> Barberry rice would be good, too.
> There aren't any barberries now.
> What are we going to do for the bridal gown?
> The groom should wear dark blue and a red tie.
> Ties are forbidden.
> Let's not forget to tell Jamal not to shave.
> I'll fix up the two rooms upstairs for them.
> It's late. Let's go to bed.
> We have to get up early to go to the airport.
> I can't sleep.
> Let's remember to take flowers to the airport.

Haji is coming, too, isn't he?
I hope Jamal approves of his bride.
Since he's been to the front and tasted bad luck, he'll be
    satisfied with anything.

GHULBACHEH: That night, nobody could sleep.   Everyone
    talked about tambourines and happiness and weddings.
    And in the morning, they got all dressed up, the father
    and mother, the women and children, the neighbors all
    set out for the airport.   At the airport there is a hubbub.
    A lot of people have come to welcome Jamal.   His Rever-
    ence and several other clerics, Guards, and Komiteh
    members stand elbow to elbow.   Suddenly, a helicopter
    appears in the sky, like a mosquito beating its wings.   It
    gets bigger and bigger, descending like an eagle and
    landing gently.   The door of the helicopter opens and
    several Guards come out, all of them grave and digni-
    fied.   The waiting crowd strains to see Jamal.   One says,
    "Jamal's the one in front."   And another says, "No, the
    next one."   Another shouts, "He's come back from the
    front.   You can't tell which one he is."   Another voice
    shouts, "What's the hurry?   Let him come forward."   But
    the brave Guards bring a box out of the helicopter and
    put it on the ground, and suddenly a number of the
    komiteh members and Guards and riffraff, who are al-
    ways present on the scene, rush to the box.   Look.   They
    lift the box to their shoulders and shout:

GUARDS' VOICES: Hey, Jamal!   Hey, Jamal!   Congratulations
    on your martyrdom!

GHULBACHEH: And suddenly, the father and mother, family
    and friends and acquaintances collapse like balloons.
    Crying and moaning rise to the sky.   Of course, they had
    a right.   Instead of their boy coming back on his own two
    feet, he had been brought back in a box.   Everyone set
    out for the city cemetery, beating their heads and chests
    and pouring dirt over their heads.   At the cemetery there
    is a strange hubbub.   The father and mother, friends and

family continually beat on their heads and chests and tear their hair, and all the others chant.

Sounds of mourning and shouting, "Our dear Jamal, flower of the revolution, congratulations on your martyrdom. You are the face of truth, the eternal light. Congratulations on your martyrdom."

Jamal's father and mother and relatives are not allowed into the mortuary. Do you know why, gentlemen? Look over here. What do you see on the mortuary slab? Hands and feet, eyes and ears, a wad of intestines, a busted skull, all jumbled up. An eye under a heal, a torn ear in the middle of intestines. And what does the mortician do? He pours a bucket of water over this mess of rotten flesh and broken bones and puts it all in a bag and gives it to the mourners, who triumphantly go to the end of the cemetery and bury the gunnysack in a hole. Jamal's family go back home, and the wedding feast becomes a mourning feast. Meanwhile, the mother and father lock horns. [*The light is lit on the faces of JAMAL'S FATHER and MOTHER.*]

JAMAL'S MOTHER [*to the FATHER*]: You murdered my child. You made him go to the front. You made him cannon fodder.

JAMAL'S FATHER [*weeping*]: I had to. What in the world should I have done?

JAMAL'S MOTHER: The same thing you should do now.

JAMAL'S FATHER: How did I know it would turn out this way?

GHULBACHEH: An elaborate memorial service begins. Pots of rice boil on the stove. Samovars bubble. Only one thing is causing the happiness. The martyr's sweets are sweet, indeed. Remember the sacks of sugar that His Reverence had sent to Jamal's father's shop? Miserable storyteller that I am, I end up reciting once again the story of the killing of Sohrab. Jamal could have escaped death, but his father killed him. The poor mother! Anyway, at night there are hordes of visitors, and Jamal's father, in order not to feel guilty, instead of a wedding party for seven days and nights, mourns for seven days and nights. And all that time people come and go. Empty stomachs enter, are filled with stew and rice and sweets, offer their congratulations and condolences, and leave. On the seventh night, suddenly a very nice car stops at the door of the house and a number of strangers enter. Nobody knows them. They go and sit in a corner. They pray for the deceased, read a chapter of the Koran, and drink tea. Some are suspicious of them. "Who are these people, already?" All the newcomers are depressed and sad. One of the newcomers says to Jamal's father, "Sir, I have a private matter to discuss with you." So they go to a quiet room and sit face to face.

The light on the canvas goes out.   ESMA'IL'S FATHER and JAMAL'S FATHER appear on stage.

ESMA'IL'S FATHER: I've come to get my son's body.

JAMAL'S FATHER: They told me my son's body was torn to bits, so how can we be sure that the body of your son was mixed with my son's?

ESMA'IL'S FATHER: Haji, if you're worried about the expense, I'll give you half in advance.

JAMAL'S FATHER: I'm thinking, how are we going to separate the bits and pieces!

ESMA'IL'S FATHER: I know my boy. Even the bits and pieces of his body, his eyes and ears and head and hands and feet. For example, on his right hand is a big mole.

JAMAL'S FATHER: They've decomposed together by now. Let's put one stone with both their names on the grave.

ESMA'IL'S FATHER: No. I want what's mine. I can't come all this way every week to pray over my child's grave.

JAMAL'S FATHER: We can't exhume a grave. It's against religious law. We'd get caught.

ESMA'IL'S FATHER: Haji, give me your consent and I'll visit the cleric and arrange it.

JAMAL'S FATHER: But...

ESMA'IL'S FATHER: But what?

JAMAL'S FATHER: But you might make a mistake and take my share.

ESMA'IL'S FATHER: Haji, I am an honorable man. I've never cheated anyone in my life. We'll sit down together, you on one side of the grave and me on the other, and we'll divide our property.

JAMAL'S FATHER [*weeping*]: I just can't bear it.

ESMA'IL'S FATHER [*weeping*]: You think I can? I just want my share. [*Both begin weeping and wailing loud and hard. The sound of their moaning becomes mixed with the weeping and wailing of men and women and the sound of praying. This crests and gradually subsides, and the stage lights slowly come up. The two fathers are no longer on stage. The light shines on GHULBACHEH.*]

GHULBACHEH: Now, look this way, please. They've exhumed the grave and brought out the bag of martyrs' rotted flesh and dumped it on the ground and started to haggle over it. It's as though they are dividing an inheritance.

ESMA'IL'S FATHER: I swear to God this is my son's hand.

JAMAL'S FATHER: No, really, it's my son's.

ESMA'IL'S FATHER: I recognize the fingernails. Didn't I tell you there was a big mole on his right hand? Look, already.

JAMAL'S FATHER: OK, then this other hand belongs to me.

ESMA'IL'S FATHER: Look at these. Are they yours or mine? For God's sake, be fair.

JAMAL'S FATHER: No, this foot belongs to you, take it. I'm not a shark.

ESMA'IL'S FATHER: Now, let's divide the ears.

GHULBACHEH: They begin to divide the ears. And at the same time, they see that instead of four ears for two people, there are five ears. One of them takes two ears and the other takes two. And the fifth ear they offer to each other.

ESMA'IL'S FATHER: Take it, it's yours.

JAMAL'S FATHER: No, my boy only had two ears. Please, you take it.

ESMA'IL'S FATHER: No, you take it, and give me that piece of intestine. [*GHULBACHEH's light comes on.*]

GHULBACHEH: In the end, Jamal's father takes the fifth ear and surrenders a length of intestine. Jamal's father pours his portion into a sack and buries it and puts a stone on the grave. And Esma'il's father puts his portion into a tub of ice. Otherwise, the foul smell of his property would make him sick during the trip home. Anyway, these two fathers go to Jamal's father's house together to say their farewells. Their hands soiled with the blood and grease of corpses, they drink a few glasses of tea with lumps of sugar on the side. Esma'il's father bargains with Jamal's father over the expenses. He pays half the funeral expenses and sets out for home. Now, let's digress a minute. [*The light of the CLERIC's face goes on.*]

CLERIC: It is necessary and required that all Moslems and believers in the Struggle of Good Against Evil not listen to the rumors of the enemy of the Islamic Republic. The only reliable source of information is our Radio of the Revolution. Now, let's listen to the news a bit. [*His hands come out of the canvas and one hand turns on the radio that is in the other hand.*]

ANNOUNCER'S VOICE: Under heavy fire, the valiant soldiers of Islam at the fronts at Sumar and Qasr-e Shirin and Khunin Shahr [Khorramshahr] have thwarted every movement of the enemy. Our fighters penetrated the enemy's territory and dispatched many of them to their deaths. According to the enemy's radio, more than fifty of the unbelievers were killed. Guard Corps Communique Number 761 announced that today more than 600 of the regime's mercenaries were captured by the Army of Islam. Our fighters today levelled the cemeteries on the outskirts of the city of Basra that had been converted to bases. Five self-sacrificing soldiers of the Army of Islam were wounded and none achieved martyrdom. [*The CLERIC turns off the radio and chuckles.*]

CLERIC: The Army of the Islamic Revolution is never defeated. it is always victorious. War, war, war till victory. [*His hands and the radio disappear behind the canvas. GHULBACHEH's light comes on. GHULBACHEH shakes his staff as he goes up and down the stage several times, then stops, facing the audience.*]

GHULBACHEH: Well, to continue our story, a week later, another car stops in front of Jamal's father's house. Several people get out, knock on the door and enter. Jamal's father is puzzled. "Who are these people, already, and where did they come from?" They sit face-to-face in a corner of the room and a thin old man takes out a piece of paper and says to Jamal's father:

OLD MAN'S VOICE: Haji, we've come from Kashan. Our son was killed at the front and his remains were brought here mixed up with your son's. I've come to get my share.

JAMAL'S FATHER [*his light is lit*]: I swear to God they came and took more than half. Nothing's left for me. All I have left is one hand and two feet, a handful of rotten intestine, and a smashed skull.

ANOTHER VOICE: Haji, just hand over our share.

UNCOUTH VOICE OF A THUG: Don't gripe, Haji, we won't leave till we get our share.

JAMAL'S FATHER: Anyone in this town will tell you that I've never cheated anyone. But I don't even know you gentlemen.

DEEP VOICE: Haji, don't force us to go to the *komiteh*. We have to exhume the body and settle the matter.

THUG'S VOICE: Come on, get up, let's go.

ANOTHER VOICE: If you don't come, we'll take it all.

ANOTHER VOICE: Shame on you. Don't try to get out of it. [*The light on JAMAL'S MOTHER's face goes on.*]

JAMAL'S MOTHER [*weeping*]: Oh, God, don't let them take my child away.

THUG'S VOICE: I'm going right now to the Guards. You seem to think we still live in the old days, when you could just grab other people's property.

FATHER'S VOICE: I'm begging you, don't do it. Look, I'll be honest with you, I have an extra ear that I can give you.

OLD MAN'S VOICE: So you were lying. When we exhume the body, maybe we'll find lots of things in it.

THUG'S VOICE: You never know, we might find some extra feet, some intestines, some jaws.

OLD MAN'S VOICE: I'll bet his head is there, too. The two feet are definitely ours.

THUG'S VOICE: We have to go to the cemetery. Come on, let's go.

To the sound of mourning, the lights on the canvas come together and light up a corner of the canvas, GHULBACHEH, his staff in hand and wearing a distraught expression, stunned.

GHULBACHEH: The father and mother, friends and family, together with the strangers, set out for the cemetery. Jamal's weeping father and mother, tears running down their cheeks, and the newcomers with happy smiles enter the cemetery. What do you think they see? See for yourselves. On every grave sits a number of people dividing their possessions. [*Sounds of chaos from men and women along with weeping and mourning, quarreling and fighting.*]

VOICE: That foot belongs to me. Hand it over.

VOICE: Why did you steal my hand?

VOICE: Don't try to hide that ear, creep.

VOICE: Why did you pick up that long intestine?

VOICE: My son's nose wasn't this big. I'm not going to let anybody cheat me.

VOICE: Take this one and give me that one.

VOICE: No, sir, I can't accept this hand. The one you got has all its fingers and this one is missing two.

VOICE: These aren't enough ribs. We learned in school that a human being has twelve ribs, and you only gave me six.

VOICE: At least give me a knee.

VOICE: All this stuff you've given me, if I put it all together, it wouldn't make a frog, much less my son.

VOICE: You think your son was the legendary Rostam?

VOICE: What I've given you is more than you deserve.

VOICE: If that foot's for sale, I might be interested.

From one side of the stage a thin, disheveled old man appears with a wheelbarrow. He circles around, shouting. A bloody cloth has been drawn over the wheelbarrow.

VENDER: Heels, knees, teeth, ribs, I've got everything. Cheap, cheap. Spleens, a burned liver, eyes and ears, pelvises, on sale. Vertebrae, good ribs, fine spines untouched by bullets. Anybody who's come up short, step right up, buy what's missing. I have good intestines, larynxes, whatever you want. I have everything, and I'll give it to you cheap. On sale, on sale. Excellent hands with or without fingers, feet in great condition, don't even smell yet. Spleens, livers, thoraxes, skulls, eyes with eyelids, good jaws. Real cheap. Come and buy. Heels, five; fine skulls, twenty. Anything you want. On sale, on sale! [*Leaves the stage on the other side. All the while the VENDER is moving around, GHULBACHEH changes positions with fear and trembling, going from this place to that.*]

JAMAL'S FATHER'S FACE [*lit up*]: After this, I'll have to mourn over an empty grave, and the sound of my crying will echo from this empty grave to that empty one. The crying of us fathers and mothers will intertwine. They came and looted and didn't leave anything for us.

CLERIC'S FACE [*lit up*]: If you want your graves to be nice and full and not mourn so much, the solution is simple. Send your other young sons to the war.

MEN AND WOMEN [*shouting together*]: There aren't any more.

CLERIC: Then, go yourselves. Become martyrs and fill the empty graves. In our Islamic Republic, nothing is impossible. If all of you can not go, some of you should go and become martyred. We'll give a portion to each person and eventually each will get a piece on the basis of Islamic equity. Haven't you ever been to a butcher shop? They sell meat to order, tenderloin and shank, heads and hooves. Whatever each person wants, we'll give him a piece of it so your graves won't be empty. Can you think of a better solution? [*The light on the canvas dims halfway, and GHULBACHEH is lit up.*]

GHULBACHEH: The city's cemeteries! All the graves empty! And everyone at the graves busy weeping and mourning. You hear soft moaning from underground. And, then what happened? We ought to listen to the radio. [*Takes a small radio out of his pocket and turns it on.*]

ANNOUNCER: Today our fighters penetrated enemy territory and dispatched many of the executioner regime's mercenaries to their deaths. Communique 1721 of our heroic army reports that many of the cemeteries outside the cities have been discovered by our valiant troops to be secret bases, which were bombed by our planes and completely annihilated. [*GHULBACHEH turns off the radio.*]

GHULBACHEH: Look over here. Helicopters bomb the grief-stricken people, and there is no longer any need to ration the bits and pieces of bodies. Body upon body piled up. [*Gives a sorrowful laugh.*] The abundance of cadavers is such that to bury them, several new cemeteries are necessary. Both sides are doing this! They're killing each other constantly in vain. They pile up the dead in vain! What have these luckless people done to deserve this punishment? Just think of the time it takes to raise a child from the time it comes from its mother's womb. [*Shouting*] Why must he be killed? Is there no cure for this calamity? No solution for this disaster? [*Pauses for a second, shouting louder.*] I ask you, is there no solution for this disaster? A senseless war, senseless wars! Must it go on like this? Won't anyone join my voice: [*Shouting louder*]   End the war, end all wars.   [*The other STORYTELLERS and the ACTORS and a number of OTHERS pour onto the stage.*]

GHULBACHEH: Enough war, enough war. Peace, peace, peace!

ACTORS AND OTHERS [*from rear of stage*]: Peace, peace, peace! [*All come to the front of the stage, the light on the canvas is cut off and there is only the shouting of the ACTORS, who repeat:*]

Enough war. Peace, peace, peace!
Enough war, enough war. Peace, peace, peace!
Enough war, enough war, enough war, enough war!
Peace, peace, peace, peace, peace!

Uses Of Otherness:
Othello In The Islamic Republic

Essay By
Kaveh Safa

At first glance, "Othello in the Islamic Republic" may appear lost, out of place. But, a longer look, I suggest, will reveal Othello to be no more lost in the Islamic Republic than he is in Shakespeare's Venice, or, for that matter, the fictive, Iranian proto-anthropologists, Usbek and Rica, are lost in Montesquieu's Paris (1961),[1] or, for that matter, the legion of Iranian princes, notables, clerics and rogues are lost in that curious genre of Iranian pseudo-histories which were but thinly disguised and transparently coded "critical" histories of contemporary French Society, Politics, Culture, and Religion,[2] or, for that matter, the mythical

---

[1] In the *Persian Letters* (1961 [1721-1758]) Montesquieu uses the voices and points of view of his fictive, letter-writing, Persians to "make strange" and obliquely criticize various aspects of French society and culture. Montesquieu, however, did not create the Persian Letters or their "uses" as a genre. Already, by 1716, a French author-lawyer, Joseph Bonnet, had landed in the Bastille for the cultural, religious, and political criticisms in his Persian Letters; and yet another Frenchman, J.F. Bernard, writing in exile (1711), had used the mask of a Persian Philosopher to point out the "barbarian" in Europeans, their characters and institutions (Van Roosbroeck 1932:61-64).

[2] According to Hadidi (1969:188-89) at their climax 51 French-"Iranian" histories were published between 1722 and 1789. In addition to the histories which used Safavid characters and events to encode and criticize contemporary French history (eg. Shah Abbas = Louis XIV; Shah Safi I = Louis XVI; Ali Homayun = Duc d'Orleans) (Hadidi 1969: 193), books on "Iranian religious history" were written to more specifically criticize contemporary religious institutions and beliefs in France. One such work by Mehegan and Gallais (1789), written ostensibly on the ancient Iranian religion of Zoroastrianism, was of enough contem-

founding-mother of story telling, Shahrazad(Sheherazade), is lost in the "Western" minds of John Barth (1972, 1984) or Luis Borges (1984).[3]

The Othello I'm referring to is the Iranian appropriation of Shakespeare's Othello in *Othello in Wonderland*, the last play to be written by the Iranian psychiatrist-playwright, Gholamhoseyn Sa`edi, before his death in exile, (Paris, May, 1985), where the play was first performed (Paris, March and April, 1985, London, April, 1985) and published (Paris, 1986).[4]

My aim in this essay is not to deny that Othello is lost in his fictive Iranian setting, but to make the point that if he is lost, he is lost with a special purpose. The special gift he bears as a stranger is his very strangeness: an actual and potential "otherness" to be "used" by his Iranian hosts to set their own house in order; an otherness "good to think with" in a totemic clash over emblems, boundaries, definitions, and classifications of the Self and the Other. My aim in this essay is to point out how, like the fictive Iranians "used" by Montesquieu and other Western writers mentioned, Sa`edi and his Iranian readers and audiences "use" the otherness of Shakespeare's Othello not to

---

porary and local relevance to bring about the imprisonment of Mehegan (Hadidi 1969: 199).

[3] I have picked Barth and Borges because of the directness of the homage they pay to Shehrezad in their fiction and critical writings. Of course, the number of such writers whose works have been directly or indirectly affected by Shehrezad and her tales is legion. To cite but a few only from England, it includes Colleridge, Beckford, Tennyson, Stevenson, George Meredith, and Charlotte Bronte— see Jassim Ali's *Shehrezade in England* (1981) for a review and bibliographic study of this fertile relationship.

[4] All my references to and quotations from *Othello in Wonderland* will be based on the 1986 edition of the play published in Paris, 1986. Only page numbers will be used for these references. A slightly different version, with lengthier initial "quotations" from Shakespeare's Othello, was a video-taped from one of the performances in London for world-wide distribution in the Iranian community-in-exile. All quotations from Shakespeare's *Othello* will be from the Chatham River Press 1984 edition of *The Complete Works of William Shakespeare*.

culturally lose themselves,[5] but on the contrary, to find themselves, as protagonists in a cultural and political contest of
immense consequence.[6]

But before examining in detail such uses of Othello, it will be
useful to draw an outline of the play, it's story line and cast of
characters, and to consider two significant non-literary

---

[5] The image of self-loss has dominated much of the recent critical
Iranian discourse on contacts and dealings with the western other. For
example, as construed by Al Ahmad in his influential book *Gharbzadegi*
or "Westernitis" (1961), given the domination and dependency that
characterizes the relationships between the West and the Third World
in economics and politics, cultural borrowings other than certain forms
of science and technology are tantamount to "catching" a fatal disease:
that is, westernitis. Other influential ideologues have elaborated
various aspects of this medical metaphor: notably Khomeini, with his
concept of *tazrigh* or "injections," making it even more agential, con-
spiratorial (Naficy 1986:3); and Khameneh'i (1986:493-5), emphasizing
the deadliness of the cultural disease, with its symptoms of self-
estrangement.

[6] Of course, Iranians are not alone in appropriating Shakespeare to
serve indigenous aesthetic and political ends. Consider, for example,
the "transgressive" or "oppositional" appropriations (Nixon 1987) of *The
Tempest* by various Caribbean and African writers, such as Cesaire in
Une Tempete (1969), Lamming in *The Pleasures of Exile* (1984), and Ngugi
in *A Grain of Wheat* (1968), in which characters and their relationships
from the *Tempest* are used to re-present the colonial and neo-colonial
situation, but as framed and valorized by the voice and point of view of
Caliban, the culturally and politically disenfranchised, protesting,
fighting back, rather than those of Prospero, the colonizer, or, as the
case might be, by his "privileged servants," "spies," and "secret police,"
represented allegorically by Ariel in Lamming's work (1984:99). The
potential for such allegorizations may in part lie on the iconic resem-
blances that Shakespeare himself drew upon to construct his images of
the Tempest, i.e. images of early colonial encounters with "natives" of
Virginia by Sir Thomas Gates (Hantman 1990, Cartelli 1987). Sa`edi's
appropriation of Shakespeare differs from these in its choice of play and
the context of its rhetoric, which is not predominantly an external
opposition, such as between colonizer and colonized, but an internal
one, between Iranians locked in conflict over issues of politics and
culture.

"environments" in the context of which the "uses" of Othello in *Othello in Wonderland* assume their rhetorical significance.[7]

Outline

The play is about the problems confronted by a secular theatrical group as it attempts to stage a performance of Shakespeare's Othello in the Islamic Republic.

To perform the play, they must obtain the permission of appropriate officials and institutions in charge of the cultural and moral welfare of the Islamic Republic. To gain this permission, they must be "inspected" by a crew of overseers, ideologues, and guardians of the Islamic Republic, for whom they rehearse various scenes of the play.

The conflicts that ensue, with potentially lethal consequences to the theatrical group, are over differences in perception and interpretation, including the religio-political status of various aspects of the play, from its authorship to its representations of wine and women. By extension, they are also conflicts over different ideas about the theater, such as regarding the boundaries between person and persona, theater and life. And by

---

[7] By rhetoric I mean the dimension of discourse that is externally "motivated" (cf. Burke 1966: 295-297), i.e., to persuade, contest, challenge, establish, question, change. Different plays or genres may capitalize on some of these ends in particular. Thus, for example, we can distinguish, as Bensel-Meyers does with regard to developments in Renaissance Drama in England, between plays dominated by an "epideictic" rhetoric of praise and blame, a "forensic" rhetoric of political and cultural fault finding, and an "elaborative" rhetoric of deliberation of culturally and historically given paradigmatic dilemmas, positions, issues (1989:71). To these types of rhetoric, all of which we find in *Othello in Wonderland*, we can add a fourth: "totemic rhetoric," the end of which is to define, establish, challenge, and defend categories of Self and Other, Us and Them, through varied associations (e.g. proprietary, emblematic), with a "third" series of similarities and differences, such as, in our case, concepts regarding the theater or meanings and interpretations regarding the particular play, Shakespeare's Othello. Cf. Levi-Strauss on Totemism (1963: 86-89), Schwartz on Cultural Totemism (1975:106-108).

further extension, they are conflicts over two views of reality, culture and politics, the chasm separating them which is recreated and brought into focus by the play's power-twisted dialogues.[8]

The course of the conflict moves in opposite directions for each side. For the theatrical group it means a descent which becomes gradually vertiginous. They begin from a position of confidence, in fact, of cultural hubris, from which they can mock and parody the boorishness, gullibility, and ignorance of their opponent. Then, they rapidly "fall" to positions of vulnerability and abjectness, in which, starting with "compromises" to save the play, soon to become "compromises" to save their necks, they become increasingly accomplices in their own "censorship," mutilating their own characters, voices and points of view to fit the values and predilections of their opponents.

Correspondingly, the latter, backed by the muscle of the state, which includes machine-gun toting Revolutionary Guards, come to increasingly engulf the discourse of the first, reshaping its meanings and forms to make them fit its own purpose and premises. Their "ascent," like the descent of the theatrical group, continues till literally the very end of the play, when there is a sudden "reversal," of which we will have more to say later.

More specifically how are the two camps constituted?

On the one side, we have the Director and actors who carry only the names of the characters they play in the play: Othello, Desdemona, Iago, Emilia, Cassio, Bianca.[9] On the other side, we

---

[8] "Twisted" because of the multi-leveled and shifting relations of domination and subordination between the participants in the dialogue, e.g. distorted by the defensive "positions" assumed by the more vulnerable partner, or the "postures" of superiority (in knowledge as well as political might) assumed by the other. To make out the patterns in these "twists," however, is not a simple task, since the positions of domination/subordination undergo many changes and reversals as we shift our focus between different levels of the play's discourse, e.g., from within the play's diegesis to its connoted but larger encompassing discourse.

[9] That the actors as characters in the play bear no names other than the characters they play in the play within the play, *Othello in Wonderland*, ironically replicates their treatment by their opponents. The actors are

have the Minister of Islamic Guidance, the Professors Khorush and Makhmalchi, a Revolutionary Guard, and his feminine counterpart, a Zeynab Sister, and a Policeman.

The two camps are symmetrical in terms of the positions their members occupy in the overall structure of the conflict between them. For example, the Director in one and the Professors in the other function as middlemen, brokers, or translators, pressing for contact and compromise—even though, ultimately unilateral, given the inequalities of power between THEM. In contrast, at the polar extremes we find the more "uncompromising" positions occupied by Othello and the Minister and his henchman.

Environment: The Theater State

The characters, their situation, and their conflicts on stage are drawn from real life. They are recognizable by their Iranian audience not only as dramatically simulated "types" (Apostolides 1988) but representations of known persons and events.

For example, the professors Khorush and Makhmalchi in the play, functioning as brokers, ideologues, and theoreticians of aesthetics and the theater for the Islamic Republic, are hardly disguised caricatures of Abdolkarim Sorush and Mohsen Makhmalbaf performing corresponding functions in the real life of the Islamic Republic.[10]

---

made to "answer" for the speech and actions of the characters they play, e.g. given a breath test for wine drinking or threatened by public stoning for sexual "immorality," by their literalist opponents who refuse to distinguish in them person from dramatic persona.

[10] Of course, these re-presentations are mediated by the play's cultural and political partisanship which is not to averse to caricaturing its targets as persons or types.   In "real life" Makhmalbaf seems to represent a more formidable and complex type of opponent than is indicated by his image in the play. Take for example two films he has made, *Dastforush* (The Peddler) and *Arusi-ye Khuban* (The Marriage of the Good [or the Blessed or the Beautiful Ones]), which have been relatively well received abroad, such as in the international film festivals of London (1988) and Locarno (Switzerland, 1989), settings which can hardly be accused of over-friendliness with the culture or politics of the Islamic Republic. The partisanship of Sa`edi's play does

Like wise, with the Islamic Republic's (to its opponents) bear-like embrace of the theater and other arts.[11] Sa`edi himself

---

not allow for the possibility that a supporter of the Islamic Republic such as Makhmalbaf can also, as indicated by these films, be a social and cultural critic. Niether does it allow for the possibility of changes in the views and works of the pro-regime film maker; or changes in the relationship itself between the film maker and the regime. Of course one can not fault Sa`edi for not divining the future: that Makhmalbaf himself would come to bear the brunt of moral, political, and cultural criticism from the regime for his pupular film script, *The Turn for Love*, sold-out in several printings despite or perhaps because of criticisms by the regime (Keyhan, 1,5,1991), and for the film he directed by the same name. Sa`edi probably would have been amused, sympathetically perhaps, at the fuss made over Makhmalbaf reducing his full beard, in congurence with post-revolutionary masculine aesthetics and decorum, to a mere over-the-lip, "full"mustache, an emblem in some Iranian quarters, of leftist or Sufi leanings, or, at least, of a parting of ways from his former political and cultural affiliations (Keyhan, ibid).

[11] Ironically, in his criticism of the Sate and its relations to the Arts, focusing on the negative effects of the State's attention as well as inattention (including hostility) to the arts, Sa`edi, writing just after the fall of the Shah (April 1979), pointed his accusing finger at the previous regime for its deleterious attentiveness to the arts. At that time he was concerned mainly with the problems of inattentiveness and/or hostility shown by the new regime towards the arts, manifested by the new censorship and destructive reactions to the theater. (1985b [1979]: 17-21.) The new regime, however, proved itself far more "interested" in the arts, especially the theater and the cinema, than Sa`edi seemed to have anticipated. Influential men rose to power with backgrounds and ongoing interests in the media. Examples of these are Prime Minster Mir Hoseyn Musavi and Fakhreddin Anvar —high official in the Ministry of Culture and Moral Guidance— both with experiences in the Shari`ati-inspired, Islamic-activist production company, formed just before The Revolution, called *Ayat Film* (Naficy 1986:21). A manifestation of the new state's interests (bear hug or not) in the theater can be seen in its sponsorship of "festivals" equally if not more impressive in scale and ambition than the festivals sponsored by the previous regime. I am referring, for example, to the annual *Fajr* Festivals, or the Regional Festival(s) of the Theater. See *Faslnameh-ye Honar* (1986) for a "critical" description of two such Festivals. More explicit manifestations of the state's interests can be found in the inaugural speeches of high ranking

provides one of the most poignant, albeit partisan, pictures of this embrace in his Theater in a Theatrical State (1984).

He depicts a process which begins with the new censorship following the execution of Sa'id Soltanpur, whose play *Abbas Aqa, a Worker at Iran National* was enjoying popular success (1984:4), and continues with ritualistic appropriations of modern Iranian secular theater, such as purification with *ab-e kor* (water as used to purify bodies polluted by sexual intercourse or nocturnal emissions before prayer or corpses before burial) of the grand hall of the Talar-e Rudaki theater in Tehran (henceforth, re-baptized Talar-e Vahdat, "Hall of Unity"), a process which destroyed expensive stage machinery by rust (Ibid. p.7). These were accompanied by "theoretical" and ideological appropriations: the imposition of new standards, models and goals for the theater, such as formulated by Makhmalbaf in his Islamic Art, which might require of the theater to convince its audience of the efficacy of Miracles (Ibid. p.6)

Little room was left for artists and works which refused this embrace, i.e. to be born again. They were excluded from any claim or role in the artistic life of the new, post-revolutionary, Iran,[12] even if they possessed such impeccable credentials of social and political commitment as did Sa'edi.[13]

---

government officials, providing encouragement and "guidance" for the theater. Such are the speeches of Hashemi Rafsanjani (Now, President of the Republic), Khameneh'i (then, President of the Republic and Leader of the High Council of the Cultural Revolution) and Moham-mad-Reza Lahuti (high official of the Ministry of Culture and Islamic Guidance) at the nation-wide Regional-Festival of the Theater and at the National Student Festival of the Theater. See the Art Quarterly, *Faslnameh-ye Honar*, for the texts of these speeches (1986: 520-521, 493-495, 540-547). All these speakers clearly "embraced" the theater as a vehicle for furthering the aims of The Islamic Revolution.

[12] By May 1979 Sa'edi was already painfully aware and protesting the continuities between the Old and New regime in their intolerance for any opposition. See his article, *"opozision" doshman nist*, or "The Opposition is Not The Enemy" (1985a [1979]).

[13] During the previous regime Sa'edi was repeatedly harassed, beaten, imprisoned and tortured for his activities as a doctor, running a free clinic with his brother for the poor and destitute in the South of Tehran,

The kind of theater to follow such cultural disenfranchisement was but a theater designed to sing the praises and justify
the ways of the new regime, a flunky theater, *ta'atr-e ta'yidi*, with
a preference for melodrama(Ibid. p.6). The flunky theater, to be
sure, existed during the previous regime, too, but, at least,
alongside it, there had come into existence a theater of protest,
ta'atr-e mota`rez, albeit self-consciously oblique and "symbolic" in
its modes of expression, as exemplified by many of Sa`edi's own
works. But this alternative theater was now totally suppressed
under the new regime of censorship (Sa`edi 1984:6-8).

By 1983 the prospects for culture and the arts in Iran seemed
bleak enough for Sa`edi to write about them in terms of "cultural
homicide" (*farhang-koshi*), what the new regime was doing with
its new regime of censorship, and "cultural suicide" (*khodkoshi-ye
farhangi*), what various publishers, writers, artists and citizens
were doing as they gave in to the censorship, self-censoring
themselves, becoming accomplices in their own cultural mutilation (Sa`edi 1983:1-6).[14]

In the every day life of the Iranian citizen this censorship
takes on a "theatrical" form. It is ironic to hear a man who had
devoted so much of his life to the theater to bemoan the rise of
the theater state, *hokumat-e namayeshi*, in which all citizens are
turned into actors and all life into a stage, *sahneh*, where citizens

---

for various of his literary activities, which included the publication of
an oppositional journal, *Alefba*, and for his refusals to "cooperate" with
the state (including its televised show-trials and rituals of recantation).
For a personal account of his arrest and prison experiences in 1974 in
the notorious Evin Prison, see his 1984 interview with Zia Sedghi, given
in London and Paris, for the Harvard Oral History Project (pp. 92-93).
For autobiographical sketches of his life, see the mentioned interview
(1984), also *Iranian Studies* 18 (1985):253-256. For a bibliography of his
works, which includes essays, ethnographies, novels, short stories, and
translations, see Southgate (1984) and *Daftarha-ye Azadi*, (1987, No. 2):
129-136.

[14] Sa`edi's own conclusion, of course, is not "cultural suicide," but its
opposite, resistance, to be waged on various fronts, especially the
aesthetic and cultural, at home and in exile (1983a: 6-7). He himself
lived up to this prescription until his death in Paris. *Othello in Wonderland* was one of his last acts of cultural resistance.

are forever destined to play roles and to be played with, as implied by the arousing slogan, *hamisheh dar sahneh*, "always on the stage/arena," in contrast to another kind of life in which, after the curtain falls, the actor ceases to be an actor. He as a human being, wipes out his make up, changes his clothes, and goes after his life. But the "always-on-stage" people have no such rights: neither to change clothes or to take off their make up. They must always follow the will of the director, which is the state, not only on stage and in front of audiences, but at home, with their wives and children, in their solitude, facing only themselves." (Sa`edi 1984:2)

Sa`edi ends his article on the *Theater State* by spelling out the theatrical stratagem to combat it. It is similar to Barthes's stratagem to combat myths with myths of myths (1972: 135-136). Sa`edi's is to create a meta-theater, a theater about the theater of the Islamic Theater (1984:9) hence the creation of *Othello in Wonderland*, a play which reappropriates the voices and points of view of its writer and audiences by re-presenting an exemplary moment in the very process of its appropriation by its adversary.

Environment: Exile

The creation of the play, however, was to be accomplished in an environment different from that of the Islamic Republic: that of exile and what Sa`edi-calls "*avaregi*" (1983:1-5)), which for lack of a better equivalent I translate as an involuntary and all-encompassing (cultural as well as social and psychological) "homelessness." *Othello In Wonderland* was staged in Paris, in March and April of 1985, and in London, in April of the same year, where the play was video-taped, to be distributed world-wide in the Iranian community. (Sa`edi died the following November in Paris).

It is unlikely that exile, this secondary environment, has not been a factor in the conception and reception of *Othello In the Wonderland*. To be sure, it is less palpable in the text of the play than the environment of the Islamic Republic. There are no explicit references to it, nor is it an explicit target of the play's rhetoric or symbolic action. To do analytical justice to the relationships between this textually distant (but I would argue experientially close) environment and various aspects of the play, we would have to take into consideration complexities of the culture-of-exile and theoretical concerns that are beyond the confines of this essay—but such as are being undertaken by Hamid Naficy (1988, 1989, 1990). It suffices my purpose to suggest a few points of possible contact and correspondence between the play and its environment of exile that will be useful to keep in mind as we study the uses of otherness in *Othello In Wonderland*.

The points concern the symbolic potentials of Othello, Shakespeare's Moor of Venice, to represent and act upon various aspects of self-estrangement and cultural disenfranchisement at "home" and in "homelessness," exile.

Consider Othello's position. Othello in Venice is a man culturally displaced—one of Shakespeare's major representations of the cultural other, the other being Shylock (Miner 1972 :94). A tragic end awaits him not only because of his vulnerability to conjugal jealousy and possessiveness, but because of a cultural otherness: an "innocence" out of phase with the games of illusion, interest, and identity, necessary for personal and political survival in Venice, so adeptly played by Yahoo. In Iago's own words, "The Moor is of a free and open nature that thinks men honest that but seem to be so and will as tenderly be led by the nose as asses are." (Act I Sc.iii)[15]

---

[15] Othello's "tragic flaw" or "errors of judgment" (hamartia), it can be interpreted, are generic to his position as the stranger. They may be linked in a simple, direct fashion to Othello being an unregenerate, barely "assimilated," "erring barbarian," under stress and in liminal situations (Cyprus vs. Venice) falling back on old "savage" ways and sentiments — as interpreted by Lawrence Olivier on stage (Honigman 1989:69-70) or Alvin Kernan in his criticism (1970). Or with greater complexity the "errors" may be linked to Othello's susceptibility as a stranger to function as a screen for projections, a lightning rod for gathering and amplifying the prejudices and contradictions of his host culture, particularly regarding gender, sexuality, and women. From this perspective Othello comes to be possessed and act out Iago's isogynist platitudes, cliches, and commonplaces about women (including mistrust and fears of infidelity), which, in turn, only articulate a deeper cultural paradigm and its contradictions (cf. Fiedler 1973: 154; Newmann 1987:145; Wiley 1989: 135; Garner 1989: 135-137; Sprengnether 1989: 196). From this perspective, as Fiedler puts it, Othello's jealousy is

Consider, also, the sentiments associated with exile. To Sa`edi, writing in exile and about his experience of exile, they include feelings of difference, innocence, vulnerability, disorientation, hopelessness, loss, mutilation, humiliation (1983). The choice of Othello as dramatic icon to somehow re-present this sense of exilic other- or othered-ness is not inauspicious. Like the "uses" of *The Tempest's Caliban* by many Third World writers, it allows for both a symbolic retelling of a distressful situation as well as (given Othello's heroic qualities, including his nobility and martial prowess) a symbolic means to protest, hit back, champion and reclaim a beleaguered Self.[16]

No less important, is Othello's potential (as play and character) to resonate with the heightened sense of reflexivity that accompanies the exile's experience of shocks, ordeals, and challenges to his or her sense of self and reality, a heightened sense of reflexivity about the contingencies and vulnerable premises (historical, linguistic, cultural, social, political...) of selfhood and otherness.

To convey this double sense of liminality and reflexivity in exile, let me quote the painful but eloquent reflections of another writer in exile, Mahshid Amirshahi, from her introduction to her novel, *Dar Hazar* (At Home), written in exile (1986).

---

not jealousy in particular but jealousy in general: the charge is against all women (1973:151, 161).

[16] To be sure, an Iranian writer or dramatist has the choice to draw on at least two indigenous narrative traditions for symbols of exile and heroic victimage: those associated with the martyrdom of the Imams in Desert of Karbela, and the story of Siyavash in the Shahnameh. But the very indigenousness of these symbols seems to militate against their usefulness as emblems to define and separate one group of Iranians from another, at least as auspiciously as Shakespeare's Othello. Sa`edi's one direct attempt to draw from the first tradition, parodying the language and form of the *ta'zieh* to caricaturize the cultural boorishness (i.e. otherness) of the play's antagonists, backfires (p.11). With non-intended irony, the parodied lines on the sufferings of being a stranger, speak directly to the fate awaiting the protagonists of the play and, by connotative extension, the situation of the play's author and audience, implied and real.

Is everyone bewildered like me? Lost like me? Sick like me? Is every one struggling? questioning? seeking? Or is it only me who spends her night in wakefulness and her day in a nightmare? Is it only me who is a stranger in her own country and an "other" among friends?... Against the revolution, among the revolution-born, is it only me?

Sometimes I think time flashes by like a shooting star, sometimes I think the world has stopped still like a heavy rock. Sometimes I see events connected together like rings in a chain, sometimes I see them like beads on a broken string, unconnected... Sometimes everything appears as if it were something else [a figure, metaphor, an allegory], sometimes it appears real... Sometimes I want to forget everything, sometimes I want nothing to escape from my memory. Sometimes rage overcomes me, sometimes shame. Sometimes fear blocks my breathing, sometimes I'm choked with tears. Sometimes I'm an observer, sometimes an actor, sometimes I submit, sometimes I rebel. Sometimes I say wait and see, sometimes I want to die and not know.

If Sa`edi and the audience of his play are twice exiled, "at home" and abroad, Othello in *Othello in Wonderland* is trice exiled: in Venice, in the theatrical repertoire of the Iranian players who have "adopted" him, and in the minds and imagination of their opponents. He is, hence, all the more prepared to re-present the trials and tribulations of his Iranian constituency-in exile.

Having looked at significant environments against which *Othello* assumes its meanings and rhetorical purpose, let us now approach the stage.

What we witness on stage is a struggle between two camps, each of which represents a distinct version of Iranianness, an Iranianness defined in terms of its relationship to Othello character, play, concepts of the theater, and ideas of society and culture implied by them. The struggle ostensibly is over the power to interpret and determine the form, meaning, and purposes of Shakespeare's *Othello*. The stakes of the struggle are high: the boundaries and coordinates of Self and Other. The prize, *Othello*, however, is also a multi-faceted instrument in this struggle. Paradoxically, it provides the two camps with a Meeting Ground for symbolic conjugations; as well as an arena for disjunctions, weapons for mutual un-selfing and othering.[17]

Othello: Conjunctions

For the two camps to engage in any form of exchange, friendly or agonistic, it is necessary for them to find a common ground of relatively shared assumptions and points of reference. A series of concepts and images, especially as they are wrenched out of their original contexts in trans-cultural translation, perform such a function in *Othello*. They are concepts and images of masculine honor, war, and blackness.

One of the main reasons why Othello can strike a sympathetic chord in the hearts of both camps is that he is a defender of masculine honor. This is one of the defenses for the Islamic legitimacy of the play provided by Professor Makhmalchi, cultural broker on the side of the Islamic Republic (pp.36-37).

His boss, the Minister of [Moral] Guidance is in fact so moved by Othello's plight and his manly resolve to murder his allegedly errant wife that he finds it difficult to contain his enthusiasm. Several times he intervenes during the course of the play on Othello's behalf.

One such occasion is provided by Othello reading his lines from Act V, Sc. II. He is torn between a sense almost of "duty" to kill his wife and a reluctance to scar "that skin whiter than snow."

---

[17] Of course, as such, the categories of Self and Other are empty forms, like personal pronouns, positions which can be assumed by different speakers in discourse (cf. Benveniste 1971: 217). But given asymmetries of power, (political, social, cultural) the categories may be in various ways "pinned" down, as well as contested, i.e., particular individuals or groups may assume a "proprietary" relationship to the category Self or may be forced or ideologically "interpellated" (Althusser 1974: 170-174) into assuming the category Other. The play represents several such contests of "selfing" and "othering" at different levels of denotation and connotation.

"...Nevertheless, she must die," he concludes, which provokes an enthusiastic outburst by the Minister. "Excellent! She must die," the Minister agrees, and in a fit of inspiration, reciting a number of edifying verses, leaps on stage, lunges at Desdemona, "like Shemr in a Ta'ziyeh performance":

> MINISTER: Oh, this whore is still here.
> Surely she should be killed,
> To guard the seed of our religion kill her now in the name of our religion. (p.42).

He intervenes again on another occasion to offer his expert advise on the best way Desdemona should be killed: by public stoning, which would be in accord with the laws of *Qisas* (punishments prescribed by Islamic Law) and would at the same time ease the husband's economic burden of having to pay "*khun-baha*" or blood money to his wife's relatives—which he would have to, if he were to kill her himself (p.44). Needless to say, Desdemona is alarmed.

Yet another meeting ground provided by the play is Othello's status as a warrior and a black person. The chain of associations invoked by these features may sound strange to Shakespeare but provide important basis for his play's hospitable reception. Thus we hear the cultural broker, Professor Khorush, justify his endorsement of Othello.

> PROFESSOR KHORUSH: Actually, in the matter of this play, I have given a favorable opinion, because of Othello himself, who was a famous commander from the land of our brothers, Morocco, and this brother Othello, like our brother Guards, was partial to war. He continually made war, believed that war was a gift from God, a blessing from God, that it was the mission of the scholars and the prophets, that a nation was made for war, everything was made for war. Othello continually fought and believed in this divine gift and blessing.(p.23)

Othello's blackness is another point in Othello's favor and the play's cultural assimilability. The chain of associations here are as follows:

MINISTER: So, he was a member of God's Army.

PROFESSOR MAKHMALCHI: I gave my approval to this drama for just that reason. Black Moslems were always prepared to go to war.

MINISTER: Yes, and let us not forget that Balal the Ethiopian, the Prophet's favorite muezzin, was black.

DIRECTOR: Naturally, Your Reverence, that is exactly why we chose this play. Othello's blackness is very important..[18] (p.23)

As the dialogue on blackness continues, the Minister is perplexed by his discovery that Othello the actor is not black, that blackness can be an illusion created by makeup, which brings in its wake doubts about the status (blackness) of the black American Hostages freed earlier from American Embassy and anger at the lack of vigilance of the officials in charge. (p.24)

The meeting grounds we have discussed so far in some way and some degree draw on Shakespeare's *Othello*, even if only in the form of signifiers to be coupled with new chains of meanings. There are others in which this point of contact is minimal or purely fictional. Striking instances of these are the religious conversions of Shakespeare and Othello.

---

[18] What the blackness of Othello means for Iranians is clearly "overdetermined." Besides the dimensions for cultural assimilation evoked by the play, there are at least two others which probably contribute to Othello's reception, albeit, indirectly, from the distance, and not "positively" for their congruence but for their contrastive tension with the images of the play. One of these is the by and large negative images of blackness found in Classical Medieval Persian Literature (Southgate 1984:3-26). The other, is the by and large positive image of blacks found in popular comic theatrical performances, taqlid and its subgenres (e.g. *ruhozi, siah-bazi, noruz-bazi*). In these plays although the black character is depicted as socially subordinate (as a *gholam* [slave] or *nokar* [servant]), he has the endearing qualities of a good-hearted trickster, often getting the better of his socially superior but mentally and morally inferior masters (Beyza'i 1966: 172-182).

Shakespeare, the "cross worshiper," is made more acceptable through the application of a traditional schema which provides him with an excuse for not being a Muslim:

> *MINISTER*: That's exactly what I said. Was this Mr. Shakespeare perhaps a follower of a sacred book?
>
> *OTHELLO*: He wrote plenty of plays, sir.
>
> *MINISTER*: I mean, was he a monotheist?
>
> *DIRECTOR*: Yes, sir, he was a Christian.
>
> *MINISTER* [*frowns*]: So, he didn't convert to Islam?
>
> *PROFESSOR KHORUSH*:   Your Eminence, Shakespeare lived before the Prophet Mohammad.
>
> *MINISTER*: Yes, yes, of course. God willing, in the next world, the Prophets and we Islamic scholars will intercede for him, and he will be forgiven. But what was the name of the play?. (p.21-22)

Othello gains even more impressive Islamic credentials through an even more circuitous chain of associations.

As the Minister discovers that brother Otughlu (Othello's name, after transcultural "translations" of semic codes (cf. Barthes 1974: 92-93), is not a brother from Azerbaijan, but from Morocco, a fellow Muslim nation with which the Islamic Republic enjoys friendly relations, he concludes:

> If that is true, then this Christian brother Shakespeare, before the appearance of His Holiness Mohammad, had received the light of Islam in his heart, and he guided brother Otughlu—may he rest his soul. (p.22)

Shortly, the Minister and his advisors concur on Othello's status as a black, Moroccan, Muslim, warrior.

Othello: Disfunctions

Let us turn now to a different set of functions assumed by Othello in the Islamic Republic. These are functions which do not create or highlight fields of congruence or convergence between the two camps, but the opposite: they oppose, separate, mark and foreground the chasms opening between the two camps, their views of the world, their cultures.

Not Understanding

The device Sa`edi uses to perform these functions is what Bakhtin, thinking of works such as *The Persian Letters* and *Gulliver's Travels*, has called the devise of "not understanding" (1981:164).

There are however important distinctions in Sa`edi's use of the device. In Montesquieu's story not understanding is the prerogative of the two strangers who applying it, or allowing themselves to become the critical instruments of their author and his audience, manage to lay bare and denaturalize the social, cultural, and political foundations of their host society.

In Sa`edi's play, not understanding, is a cognitive and emotional posture not associated with the heroes but the villains. It is less an instrument for gaining critical insight than for "othering" the Other, for defining and debasing him in opposition to the Self. A certain kind of cultural knowledge, eg. of Shakespeare, Othello, and secular theater in general, is what differentiates "Us" (author/the play's protagonists/ sympathetic audience) from "Them."[19] At the same time, the Other's emblematic igno-

---

[19] That "proprietary" relation of the secular theatrical group towards Shakespeare's Othello is not without its justification, given the place already occupied by this play in the world of modern Iranian theater, as indicated by the play's numerous translations. Thus in his history of dramatic literature in Iran Malekpur (1984:283-292) is able to critically compare three major translations of Othello: by Naser ol-Molk (published in 1961), Behazin (published in 1971), and Nushin (published in 1978). Incidentally, given our earlier discussion of exile, oppositional artistic-cultural activity, and choice of *Othello* as icon and symbolic weapon..., all three translators share with Sa`edi prolonged

rance is not merely an empty or passive state. It is animated by the dynamics of power. It is a militant ignorance, which attempts to appropriate the symbols and meanings of the Other through various forms of mis-translation, with results that are, from "Our" vantage point, comically absurd, and,   given the power behind them to define and impose their definition of reality, frighteningly grotesque. Let's look at specific examples.

The play opens with displays of casual mastery of the symbolic world of *Othello* by members of the theatrical group: smoking, knitting (Desdemona), chatting, weaving in and out of their roles, as they joke and tease each other about their roles, from vantage points inside and outside them (pp.3-6). By the time the Director enters the scene, with permit in hand (after five months trying) for the play's performance, little doubt is left as to who is in the know—and who is not. "Didn't I tell you, I could fool them [i.e. make them, the government authorities, believe anything]," the Director declares, with, unjustifiable cultural hubris.

The permit he displays is a testament to their opponents' ignorance, cultural incompetence. It allows the company "to stage the Elizabethan play Shakespeare by Othello"(p.8)

This state of not-understanding is confirmed by the Minister, soon after he makes his appearance on stage. In a highly stylized manner —Sa`edi's parody of clerical learned discourse— he pontificates:

> MINISTER: Yes, yes, of course. A great writer. Of the same stature as the well-known French Islamicist, Walter. In one of his histories, maybe his "Punishments and Retributions," I read that Gustave Le Bon in his famous book, "Falamarian," greatly praised the man and rated him as among the greatest of thinkers. He wrote a book entitled [to KHORUSH], do you happen to recall the title? (p. 21)

experiences of exile (the first in England, the second in the Soviet Union, both for political reasons) activism (Behazin, in the Iranian left).

Khorush, answers, "Perhaps *'Committed Art and Discord in Noncommitted Art'*," adding a string of nonsense words, supposedly in English (p.21).

As the play continues, such disjunctures, in which Othello is used as a cultural totem to define and differentiate the two groups multiply.

Mis-Translations

At one deceptively simple level, brought into focus by comical and occasionally grotesque mis-translations, *Othello* provides an arena for a battle over names and other synechdochic representations, saturated with cultural and ideological connotations Barthian terminology, a battle over the "semic" code.[20]

At stake might be the forms and connotations of proper names: e.g., Othello vs. Otughlu, Desdemona vs. Desdamama; Cassio vs. Casico; Bianca vs. Binekah. The boorish distortions for one camp are but acts of cultural assimilation in the other.

The nominal transformations are congruent with deeper transformations of character and function as they are subjected to applications of different moral, political, and aesthetic codes. We have already seen such a transformation with regard to Othello. To it we can add Iago's transformation to a pimp, bastard and counter-revolutionary (p.33); Bianca (Cassio's lover) to recalcitrant whore (p.30); and Cassio to a penitent, ex-*monafeq*

---

[20] Barthes (1974:94-95). To stress the significance of miss-translating names, let me quote Silverman drawing on Barthes's *S/Z* to discuss the significance of the "semic code": "The semic code represent the major device for thematizing persons, objects, or places. It operates by grouping a number of signifiers around either a proper name, or another signifier which functions temporarily as if it were a proper name."(1983:251)..."In conjunction with cultural codes...[it defines] person and place in ideologically symptomatic ways. On the significance of Iranian naming practices, especially the conferring of "non-Islamic," ancient Iranian, as opposed to Islamic names in recent Iranian political and cultural history, see Roy Mottahedeh (1985: 312-331). For a discussion of the pragmatics of naming and name-changing among Iranian immigrants in the U.S., see Betty A. Blair (1987).

(label for a *mojahed*, member of the Mojahedin-e Khalq, the guerrilla organization) (p.26).

Even Shakespeare and some of his characters outside *Othello* are not immune to these nominal and deeper translations. Thus professor Makhmalchi informs us of his book in progress which proves that Shakespeare was a Bedouin Arab, named Sheikh Zobeyr, whose name and works were and still are altered by Estekbar-e Jahani [World Imperialism] (pp.36-37). He also tells us what Sheykh Zobeyr intended to prove in his play known by the name of *Romeo and Juliet*, but which is in fact, *Rahim and Raheleh*: namely, that the love between Romeo and Juliet "soars" *after* they are married, but is opposed by their families who are firm believers in prostitution (moral corruption) *namzadbazi* [pre-marital courtship associated with "engagement"](p.36).

The locus of cultural mistranslation can also be labels, terms of reference, address, poetic metaphors, and objects.

Thus an accidental reference to Cassio having a "lover," *ma'shuqeh*, is enough to provoke a major disturbance, promising dire consequences for Cassio and Bianca, who are offered but refuse the Minister's solution of a "temporary marriage", *sigheh*, on stage (p.30). Likewise, Othello addressing his wife as *nazanin-e man*, "come my dear love" (Act II, SC. iii), rather than more culturally appropriate terms such as "woman of the house," "privates," "weakling," provokes a lecture by the Minister on West-strickenness and corruption (p.32). He begins to call Desdemona "My woman of the house..."

Terms of address, too, may need re-translation because of their social and political encoding. Thus the director must not address the actors as "friends," (cf. comrade) which, the Revolutionary Guard screams, is what Communists say, but, more appropriately, "brothers and sisters." (p.39) Even the order in which classificatory terms for siblings are used must be changed to strictly follow the rules of sexual hierarchy in the new political order. "Sisters and brothers," is wrong, it misplaces priority. The corrected form is,"brothers and sisters." (p.40)

Objects too are not immune to translation. For example, Othello's handkerchief, the Minister insists, "is wrong." What Desdemona, the adulteress who is also given to praying, has given Cassio, her lover, must be her [Othello's gift] *sajjadeh*, prayer rug. Thus Othello is forced to translate his line to: "By heaven, with my own eyes I saw Cassio praying on the prayer rug I gave you," (p.43) which brings to Minister's mind the double complicity of "these *monafeq*s," since "first they commit adultry on a rug, and then they pray on it." And he spits in disgust.(p.44).

No less significant in terms of its connotations are Othello's poetic references, in a song overheard by Desdemona and Emilia, to his "sword of Spain, the ice-brook's temper."(p.46) Professor Makhmalchi cracks their dangerous encoded message.

> *PROFESSOR MAKHMALCHI*: I object. This kind of talk is that of Hypocrites. They have songs. "Canst thou hear" is a code. The weapon in the brook is an allusion to a guerilla operation.

> *OTHELLO*: This was written several centuries ago. What does it have to do with guerilla operations?

> *MINISTER*: Yes, the seeds of discord were sown in those days. Islam was hindered by the Hypocrites right from the beginning. The Hypocrites are worse than infidels, the Great Satan. Satan has existed from the beginning of time. The Great Satan means these ideas. It means rejecting. [*To KHORUSH*] What do they call it?

> *PROFESSOR KHORUSH*: Code.

> *MINISTER*: Yes, coat.

> *PROFESSOR KHORUSH*: Meaning, to talk in code, secretly, with signs.

> *MINISTER*: No, sir, this play, Mr. Othello, or whatever, which pretends to be Islamic, definitely has had contact with global oppressors, even international Zionism.. (p.46)[21]

---

[21] Among other coded, hence, contested emblems are: perfumes = *taghut* (Corrupters, Oppressors, i.e. the elite of the Old Regime) (p.35); and *kakh* (Palace, also emblem of *taghut*) translated and culturally reconstituted as *kukh* (Slum, supposedly championed by Khomeini).(p.31)

Theater as Totem

It is not only details such as we have examined that function as emblems and symbolic instruments for defining and separating categories of the Self and Other, but the theater itself. In fact, at the core of *Othello in Wonderland* is a meta-theatrical discourse about the theater which imbricates oppositions regarding how the theater is viewed and experienced (e.g. regarding relationship between life and dramatic re-presentation, between actor and role) with oppositions between the Self and Other.

Of this metatheatrical discourses we find two basic forms. One is a "naive" form, not explicitly voiced or elaborated, to be "read," for example, from the reflex-like reactions of the inarticulate Revolutionary Guards. The other is self-consciously ideological or theoretical, such as voiced by the professors Khorush and Makhmalchi. (Of course, these forms are neither discrete or unique to one camp or character).

Metatheatrical Discourse: The Naive Form, Literalism

Let us look at the naive form first. The play's opening scene (3-6) of actors chatting, smoking, knitting, joking, dozing, literally playing with their roles, casually juggling self and dramatic persona, switching back and forth between theatrical discourse (marked, among other things, by a stilted, Shakespearean Persian) and the discourses of ordinary life (e.g. about work, fatigue, back aches (p.4)), clearly displays an understanding of the theater in which person and persona and life and its theatrical representations are viewed as distinct but capable of mutual commentary and interpretation.

The bared back stage images with which the play begins establishes Sa`edi's subscription to a modernist view of the theater in which, like Brecht's, the objective of the theater is not to create and maintain theatrical "illusions," but the opposite, to use the transparently illusory representations to create cultural and ideological "seismic" shocks (cf. Barthes on Brecht, 1986: 214), cracks in the status quo views of reality, to produce reflexivity and insight.

This understanding of the theater voiced and acted out by members of the theatrical company puts them on a course of multiple collisions with their antagonists. One important point where such collisions occur concerns the "literalism" with which theatrical "illusions" are experienced or acted upon. The Revolutionary Guard and the Zeynab Sister are die-hard literalists.[22]

Thus if "Desdemama" is an adulteress, the Minister threatens to have her stoned to death, right on stage (p.44). If Binekah and Casico (in real life with wife and child) are lovers in the play, the actors must be married (with a temporary marriage) on stage (p.30). If Iago makes a reference to wine (p.34), the ever vigilant evolutionary Guard must find the jug of wine and administer breath tests to the suspicious actors.

It makes little difference to Revolutionary Guard if, as the Director explains, "there is no jug involved. They have drunk wine in the drama [deram]." (p.34)

> REVOLUTIONARY GUARD: It makes no difference to me where they drank it, Cafe Deram, Cafe Kowkab, Aqa Reza Soheyla, whatever. [Goes to OTHELLO.] Go "huuuh." (p.34).

From this perspective, art has to answer to life in no uncertain terms (with the life of the artist at stake). Thus, earlier, when the director, following the new "ideologically correct" typology of dramatic characters (p.25), introduces Iago as a "counter-revolutionary," the Revolutionary Guard reacts spontaneously, pulls out his gun and orders him, "hands up."

---

[22]. Their literalism is but an extreme manifestation of their "non-understanding," attesting to a "mythical" mode of thought and "mythologized" experience of the world, which White describes in terms of an "inclination to take signs and symbols for the things they represent, to take metaphors literally, and to let the fluid world indicated by the world of analogy and simile slip its grasp." (1972:33) It is important to remember, however, that the literalism that the play ascribes mainly to its antagonists is itself part of a rhetoric which mythologizes its adversaries.

In self defense Iago (the actor) must prove his revolutionary "credentials" to the Guard. A cycle of revolutionary boasts, counter-boasts, and testimonials ensues.

> IAGO [*flustered and frightened, raises his hands*]: Me a counterrevolutionary? Not me, during the revolution I took part in every march.
>
> REVOLUTIONARY GUARD [*moves forward menacingly*]: What did you do during the revolution, for example?
>
> IAGO: The same things everybody did.
>
> REVOLUTIONARY GUARD: I broke fifty bank windows by myself, like the Imam commanded. How many did you break?
>
> IAGO: Fifty-one.
>
> DIRECTOR [*stepping in*]: It's true, brother, I saw him, I give you my word of honor.
>
> REVOLUTIONARY GUARD [*to IAGO*]: How many movie theaters did you set fire to?
>
> IAGO: Me set fire to a theater?
>
> REVOLUTIONARY GUARD: I knew you were a counterrevolutionary.
>
> DIRECTOR: I swear to God, he's not a counterrevolutionary.
>
> REVOLUTIONARY GUARD [*to the DIRECTOR*]: You said he was one yourself, didn't you?
>
> DIRECTOR: No, brother, he's imitating one. (pp.25-26)

In response, the Revolutionary Guard, formulates his most reflexive statement on poetics: "If someone imitates something, that's what he is." (p.26)

Literalism, however, is not unidirectional: it does not move only from life to art. Not only can it "dissolve" art in life, such as we see in the Revolutionary Guard's confidence that incriminating records on Othello can be found in the documents captured at the American Embassy, that is, after the Minister has discovered the links between Othello and World Imperialism and International Zionism. But art can spill over into life, with important consequences.

Consider the effects on the Minister of a heightened awareness of theatrical artifice, for example, of the possibility that that skin color on stage may be an artificial creation. The effect is not a weakening of his literalism, but a shift of target, a literalist application of a knowledge of theatricality to life. He complains that in order to make sure the Black Hostages freed from the Nest of Spies [occupied American Embassy] were *really* black [not made-up blacks like Othello] they should have been taken to the bath and given a good scrub (p.24). To prevent such dangerous negligence to occur again he plans to make the appropriate recommendations to the government.

Literalism, we also stress, is not merely the prerogative (or liability) of only one side. It occurs occasionally among members of the theatrical company. But this is a "reactive" literalism, clearly linked to the latter's sense of vulnerability and disorientation in facing the unpredictable and "incomprehensible" literalism of their opponents, who increasingly hold power over their lives and definitions of the real and unreal.

Thus the actors (with the exception of a mocking Othello) are agitated by the medical metaphors Khorush uses in one of his pontifications on disease, diagnosis and therapy in the arts, evoking images of urine analysis and the enema (for diagnostic testing and therapy of the arts/artists, to which we shall return later). As he stops, a worried Iago asks: "What does it mean? They want to take our urine?" And Cassio, stricken with anal anxiety, declares, "I won't let them give me an enema!" (p.20).[23]

---

[23] To the literalisms of the theatrical group we can add a literalism of the author and his implied sympathetic audience: a seemingly unproblematic understanding of and identification with Shakespearean theater, as if it were primordial, unitary, and uncontested in form, meaning, ideology, and "use." What this literalism precludes is a

To comfort them, the minister pulls back his cloak, under which they can see he is not hiding any instruments for urine analysis or the enema. The members of his entourage, too, he assures them, are carrying naught in their bags but books for moral guidance (p.21).

Metatheatrical Discourse: Theories of the Theater

Beyond distinctions theatrical oppositions between life and art, *Othello in Wonderland* uses differences in theories about the theater to define and distinguish the two camps.

The theories of one camp, secular and modernist are "acted out" early in the play. They provide a contrastive background against which the other side articulates its own theories and criticisms of the theater.

The theorists in this camp are the Minister and his two professorial advisors. Soon after their first encounter, the Minister makes it known that Drama, like post-coital ritual purifications, must meet certain conditions, of which, evoking the image of the three legs of a three-legged stool, there are three (p.17).

---

consideration of the possibility that even in England and the "West" Shakespeare's theater has been in a process of constant re-invention, re-interpretation, and re-valuation (cf. Taylor 1989; Howard 1987, Charney 1988); and that the terms of the contests over various aspects of the plays have not always been radically different than those satirized by Sa`edi in his play. To consider but a few examples, we can refer to the problems of "Bardolatry" (Charney 1989:18), or "Shakesperotics," which Taylor defines as "[embracing] everything that a society does in the name—variously spelled—of Shakespeare."(1989:6). We can refer to the debates on the blackness of Othello, (Newmann 1987) much of it no less absurd or consequential than those conjured by the Iranian play; or to debates, fueled by religious fervor, over theatrical artifice, especially with regard to cross-gender acting (Sprengnether 1989), debates which would only warm the hearts of Sa`edi's clerics with their familiarity; or we can refer to political applications of Shakespeare (e.g. Henry V) for "patriotic purposes" or political propaganda, with the text of the play, like Othello in Sa`edi's play, being open to ideological appropriation by both sides, British and German at war (Hawkes 1988:59).

After a circuitous discussion in which the Minister displays his knowledge of Aristotle (=Aristo=Stotles) and his materialist theories of divination (p.17), he spells out the three "legs":

> ...because our drama, like our revolution, must be exported to every part of the world. Therefore, in the end, a true Moslem must give up his life, sacrifice his blood, everything he has. That is, he must be one of God's soldiers, so that the great tree of the Revolutionary Islamic Republic is fruitful. An apostate or polytheist or, worst of all, a Hypocrite, is punished for his evil deeds.
>
> In addition to ransoms and fines and lashing and stoning and revolutionary execution, on Judgment Day, the fate of such people will be revealed and become a warning and a lesson to others. Now, as to the third leg of the tripod, it is to show repentance, how the light of faith shines in their hearts, as a result of guardianship under the influence of the Brothers, how they come out of prison and join the brotherhood of the faithful. But, of course, it is necessary in drama for the repentants to always feel humiliated, embarrassed, to always keep one's head lowered, to be modest and contrite about one's past. And in drama, too, repentance must not be neglected. Several self-sacrificing Guards must always watch over them so that they do not stray from the Islamic line into the Hypocrites' groups and establish safe houses.(p.18).

An immediate application of this theory is a characterological "re-fitting" of the play in which Iago is identified as the counter-revolutionary (p.26), Cassio as the suspiciously penitent *monafeq* (p.26), and Othello, as the manly black Muslim warrior (p.23).

The translations however prove themselves to be unstable, the molds fail to hold the characters. For example, Othello in his fall from grace becomes not only a haughty *taghuti* (identified by the label with the corrupt and oppressive elite of the Pahlavi Era), a dangerous code-passing *mojahed*, an agent of World Imperialism and Zionism, but an adulterous necrophiliac (pp.46-48) — in all, a shameless violator of the first "leg."

Two other theoretical statements complement the Minister's model of correct Drama, one focusing on questions of goals and motives, the other on standards and applications.

According to Professor Makhmalchi, art is an instrument for propaganda, that is, propaganda serving the high goals of the Islamic Republic.(p.19) Using frugiferous metaphors, he pontificates on the significance of goals.

> *PROFESSOR MAKHMALCHI*: ... we must understand that a peach pit is really a peach pit in order to eat the peach.
>
> *OTHELLO*: But until you've eaten the peach, you can't see the pit.
>
> *PROFESSOR MAKHMALCHI*: Revolutionary art, sir, must above all consider political and ideological content. The edible part of the peach itself is not a consideration. On page 104 of my book, I suggest that, in the writer's words, it is not necessary and has no role in the general progress of a story and must not be used. What do I mean by progress? What? The pit of the peach. The ideological-political pit of the issues.
>
> *OTHELLO*: So the only value of a peach is its pit?(p.39)

Professor Khorush's choice of metaphors in his theories about the ideological testing and reforming of the arts are even more provocative. We touched upon them earlier, but they bear closer scrutiny.

The key metaphors professor Khorush are *qarureh gereftan*, which he explains, "was a practice of the ancients in their laboratories. Today, we would term such a sample a urine specimen. They could diagnose a disease solely by the sediment in urine and its color and smell"; and *emaleh*, or the enema. He explicates:

> Now, an enema is the apparatus that is inserted into the rectum and a liquid flows into it so that a patient is treated and cured. Therefore, in our Islamic Republic, two subjects must be brought up. We must get urine specimens from artists to determine what illnesses they have.

As Othello bursts out in mocking laughter, the professor continues,

> Wait, Mr. Othello, look at the revolutionary aspects of
> this matter. If we get urine samples, we won't have
> artists who are supporters of the Tyrant, or Hypocrites,
> or Communists. It absolutely wouldn't be censorship.
> It's a medical procedure, so we definitely must get
> samples. And brown sugar enemas, for which ancient
> medical books praise their properties, stop fever, bring
> psychological and spiritual health, and would bring
> strength and health to our Islamic Republic. Brown
> sugar enemas for the purpose of ideological-political
> guidance will help us resist the global oppression of the
> East and West. In the case of theater arts, they are nec-
> essary, in other words, a responsibility.(p.20)

The more the ordeal-masters "testing" Othello for its ideological and Islamic correctness spell out their theories, the more
clearly are established the irreconcilability of differences between
the two sides.

Attempts at reaching a "compromise" only further accentuate
this irreconcilability, unless it is at the cost of catastrophic
mutilations to be suffered by the beleaguered side in its views
and values especially as they are embodied in Othello.

Consider, for example, Khorush's attempt to break the
deadlock of the rehearsal-ordeal. He tries to rehabilitate Shakespeare and his creation by associating him in a dream-like
"compromise" with Hafez, whose credentials are impeccable and
whose divan, book of poems, enjoys respect not only for the
aesthetic and philosophical pleasures it provides but for its
bibliomantic, divinatory functions.

The logic of his associations runs as follows:

> With no offense to the great poet Hafez, who memo-
> rized the entire Koran, Shakespeare can be considered
> the Hafez of his time. For centuries people have re-
> solved their problems through faith in divination using
> Hafez's poetry. Now we should practice divination
> with drama to see what Shakespeare tells us..(p.37).

But the attempt at compromise backfires. The book "opens"
inauspiciously to ACT II, SC. iii, to Iago bearing false witness to
Othello about his wife's unfaithfulness, reporting to him what he

has heard Cassio say and do while asleep, obviously "recollecting" in his dream a scene of illicit love-making with Desdemona. "Sweet Desdemona/ let us be wary, let us hide our loves" (p.38). The lines only provide evidence for the prosecution, against the play and its characters (=actors).

Similarly, as Khorush and the Minister try to give the other side a very last chance, it can only take the form of a radical mutilation of Othello, of the play's form in time. The Professor suggests and the Minister elaborates a macabre analogy between the theater and chickens. Why not start the play at its end?

> MINISTER [*knitting his brow*]: I have no objection. Actually, I've read that His Holiness Sadeq has been reported to say it is better to start a drama from the end. In fact, as the saying goes, "What do they do with the chicks after they hatch?"
>
> OTHELLO [*sarcastically*]:They count them and eat them. (p.36)

The Minster laughs, and his laughter ripples down the pyramid of power. The professors laugh. The Revolutionary Guard laughs.

As the play approaches its climax, it is clear the chasm that has opened up between the side is unbridgeable. Even the director who earlier in the play had boasted he could make asses of the other side, now tries to throw-in the towel. With the rest of his troop, he has become painfully aware of their powerlessness and vulnerability. He wants out, he wants to disengage (p.35), but his opponents will not let go, like sadistic cats refusing to relinquish their terrorized, half-dead prey.

Previously they had pontificated at length on the "potentialities" of the arts and the theater (for Islam and the Revolution). Now they insist on corrective surgery, which means cutting out whole scenes, as well as "reforming" characters and actors.(p.36)

The Reversal

The climax of the play is a surprise, a reversal. Othello, representing several levels of cornered Self (Sa`edi, the players, the audience), cuts through the several frames separating art from life. Here Sa`edi's indulges in his one flagrant departure from Shakespeare's play, transforming Othello's suicide to a symbolically saturated homicide, an act of outward aggression the target of which is obvious to most Iranians.

Where Shakespeare's Othello, invoking the image of a "malignant Turk" says:

> ...Set you down this; and say besides, that in Aleppo once, Where a malignant and turbaned Turk Beat a Venetian and traduced the state, I took by the throat the circumcised dog, and smote him thus. (stabs himself) (ACT V, SC. ii)

Sa`edi's Othello says:

> (dramatically) and say this, too, that, one day, I saw a turbaned man, a pretender, false prophet, abusing [every thing that was good and decent]. I called to my companions, and I approached him. I took the cursed dog's throat and struck him thus (as he draws Iago's sword from its scabbard and attacks the Minister, the stage lights flicker on and off and play ends). (p.48)

Conclusion

The light goes out, freezing the motion of the sword. But the sword arm of Othello has a momentum which doesn't stop at the boundaries of the play. We can trace its virtual trajectory as it cuts through the turbaned skull of the Minister, the cultural and political nemesis of Othello, magically spilling art into life, the wished for imaginary into the real.

The same movement, however, makes more visible the rhetorical motor that has motivated the polyphonic and multi-leveled discourse of the play, a motor with a double motion, driving the play towards two different "conclusions": One, at the surface-level of unfolding story-line, moving it towards a night-marish conclusion in which characters epitomizing cultural and political otherness ultimately engulf and crush the reality of the self by appropriating its emblem, Othello; the, other, on a more implicit, connotative, level, moving the play towards conclusions in which many of the relationships of domination and subordi-nation in the first are inverted, particularly with regard to powers of definition (of self and other) and powers of allocating positions of subject and object in the discourse of the play.

At the level of the play's story-line, the most directly visible rhetoric is that which shapes it as an acted out myth of victimage (cf. Girard 1978). The "yield" of this rhetoric, to the extent that it is successful, is to "make" the audience sympathize or identify with the positions of the victim, which they find, correspond-ingly to represent themselves, as victims of the politics and culture of the Islamic Republic, victims of internal and external exile. The victim's rage is but followed by the victim's revenge, in which "we" the sympathetic audience also become accomplices. Othello's sword arm, thus, does not belong to him only, but to "us" as well, an "us" which includes the real and implied author of the play and its real and implied audience.

Othello's violence, reminiscent of the ritualized murder of Omar in effigy in Iranian rituals of *Omar Koshun* [Omar Killing), is but an irruption of a generally more subtle kind, a self-centered and self-serving rhetoric of violence which engages the Other in deadly combat throughout the play. To understand its "ends" one has to "read" it backwards from the surface diegesis of the play, reverse its chain of cause and effects. If we do this, we become aware of how much this combat is "fixed" in favor of the Self — despite or in opposition to how things are represented on the surface level or "exist" out there in the "real" world with its different balance of power. The rhetoric at this level uses the myth of victimage (self as sacrificial victim) to "set up" the other-as-victimizer, preparing him for his just and deserved sacrifice, in the space of the play or its virtual extensions. The nightmarish rise of the Other (at the expense of the Self) in the play but places him on the edge of an abyss down which, given his demon-strated moral, cultural and political worthlessness, he deservedly will tumble. Othello's sword provides but the initiatory nudge.

However, even without it, on the level of more subtle connotations of the play, the outcome of the contest is reversed as to
who has the power to define whom, who has the power to draw
boundaries, allocate positions of selfhood and otherness.

Even as on the surface level of the play's diegesis its
"antagonists" appear to be un-selving the Self by appropriating
its emblem, mutilating and recasting Othello to fit their own
standards and values, the play is turning the tables on them. The
very same actions which demonstrate their power to dominate,
in the deeper and more over-arching rhetoric of the play, contribute towards their transformation to ideological caricature,
their ultimate definition as the Other.

On the surface level the Other can out-shout the voices of the
Self. But his own voice, ultimately, does not belong to him.
Grotesquely stylized, predictable, formulaic—it is the voice of
the ventriloquist's dummy. Like wise, he may be imposing his
point of view on the Self, but his eyes, in the larger discourse of
the play, are blind, blinded by "non-understanding" and preju-
dice (of the wrong sort, i.e. not belonging to the Self). In other
words, the play does to the Other as villains of the play as the
villainous Other does to the Self: it "speaks them," they become
its "spoken subjects."

Let us hear once more the voice of the dramatist in exile
reflecting on the estrangements of exile at home:

> ...Words and language are the tissue and texture of
> the theater... If I am in a corner of the world where I
> don't understand the language of its people, I under-
> stand that I don't understand. But if I am somewhere
> where they are speaking in the language that I know
> and I absolutely don't understand anything, I think
> I've been stricken by a nightmare or madness.
> (1984:p.8)

Given this nightmare, we can appreciate the gifts Othello
bears his Iranian hosts: a mother-like mirror which with the
rhetorical and ideological warps of its reflecting surface allows a
besieged and disintegrating Self to find and reconstitute itself;
also a symbolic weapon to "hit back" at the forces which politi-

cally, culturally and aesthetically engulf it and are pulling it apart, in other words, a weapon to "other the Other."

REFERENCES

Ale-e Ahmad, Jalal. 1961. *Gharbzadegi* [Westernitis]. Tehran.

Althusser, Louis. 1971. "Ideology and Ideological State Apparatuses," in *Lenin and Philosophy and Other Essays*, by Louis

Althusser. New York: Monthly Review Press.

Amirshahi, Mahshid. 1987. *Dar Hazar* [At Home].

Apostolides, Jean-Marie. 1988. "Moliere and the Sociology of Exchange." *Critical Inquiry* 14, pp. 477-492.

Bakhtin, Mikhail. 1981. *The Dialogic Imagination: Four Essays by M.M. Bakhtin*. Tr., Caryl Emerson and Michael Holquist, ed.,

Michael Holquist. Austin: University of Texas Press.

Barth, John. 1972. "Dunyazadiad." In John Barth, *Chimera*. New York: Random House, 1972.

Barth, John. 1984. *The Friday Book: Essays and Other Non-Fiction*. New York: G.P.Putnam's Sons.

_____. 1974. S/Z. Richard Miller Tr. New York: Hill and Wang.

_____. 1975. *Mythologies*. New York: Hill and Wang.

Barthes, Roland. 1986. "Brecht and Discourse: A Contribution to the Study of Discursivity." In *The Rustle of Language*, by Roland Barthes. New York: Hill and Wang.

Benveniste, Emile. 1971. *Problems in General Linguistics*. Tr., Mary Meek. Coral Gables: University of Miami Press.

Beyza'i, Bahram. 1966. *Namayesh dar Iran* [The Theater in Iran].

Blair, Betty. 1987 "Iranian Name Changes in Los Angeles: The Immigrants' Quest for Security and Power in a New World." M.S. University of California at Los Angeles.

Borges, Jorge Luis. 1984. "The Thousand and One Nights." *Georgia Review* (1984):464-574.

Burke, Kenneth. 1968. *Language as Symbolic Action*. Los Angeles: University of California Press.

Cartelli, Thomas. 1987. "Propsero in Africa: The Tempest as Colonialist Text and Pre-Text." In *Shakespeare Reproduced: The Text in History and Ideology*, edited by Jean Howard and Marion O'Conner. New York: Methuen.

Cesaire, Aime. 1969. *Une Tempete: D'Apres "la Tempete" de Shakespeare — Adaptation pour un theatre negre*. Paris.

Charney, Maurice, ed. 1988. *"Bad" Shakespeare: Revaluations of the Shakespeare Canon*. Rutheford: Farlieh Dickinson University Press.

Fiddler, Lease. 1972. *The Stranger in Shakespeare*. New York: Stein and Day.

Garner, Shirley Nelson. 1989. "Male Bonding and the Myth of Women's Deception in Shakespeare Play." In *Shakespeare Personality, edited by Norman Holland*, et. al. Berkley: University of California Press.

Girard, Rene. 1978. "Violence and Representation in the Mythical Text." In *To Double Business Bound: Essays on Literature, Mimesis and Anthropology*, by Rene Girard. Baltimore: Johns Hopkins University Press.

Hadidi, Javad. 1969. *Iran dar Adabiat-e Faranseh* [Iran in French Literature]. Mashad: Mashad University Press.

Hantman, Jeffrey. 1990. "'Caliban's Own Voice': Seeking Native Views of the Other in Colonial America." Presentation at panel discussion on *The Cultural Other: Cross Cultural Profiles*, at the Commonwealth Center For Literary and Cultural Change, University of Virginia, Charlottesville.

Hawkes, Terence. 1988. "Wittgenstein's Shakespeare." In *"Bad" Shakespeare: Revaluations of the Shakespeare Canon*, edited by Maurice Charney. Rutheford: Farlieh Dickinson University Press.

Honigmann, E.A. 1989. *Myriad-Minded Shakespeare*. New York: St. Martin's Press.

Jassim Ali, Muhsin. *1981 Scheherazade in England: A Study of Nineteenth-Century English Criticism of the Arabian Nights*. Washington: Three Continents Press.

Kernan, Alvin. 1970 "Othello: An Introduction." In *Essays in Shakespearean Criticism*, edited by James Calderwood and Harold Toliver.

Khameneh'i, Ali (Hojjat-ol-Eslam). 1986-1987. "Rosukh va Gostaresh-e Mafahim-e Enqelabi dar Honar-e Namayesh Yek Niaz-e Mobram Ast" [The Spreading of Revolutionary Ideas in The Art of Theatre is a Pressing Problem]. *Faslnameh-ye Honar*, pp. 493-495.

Khatami, Mohmmad (Hojjat-ol-Eslam). 1986-1987. "Natijeh-ye Jashnvareh-ha-ye Mantaqeh'i Mardomi Kardan-e Honar-e Ta'atr Ast" [The Product of The Regional Festivals is the

Popularization/de-Elitization of The Art of the Theater]. *Faslnameh-ye Honar*, pp. 522-531.

Lamming, George. 1984. *The Pleasures of Exile*. New York: Alison and Busby.

Levi-Strauss, Claude. 1963. *Totemism*. Tr. Rodney Needham. Boston: Beacon Press.

Malekpur, Jamshid. 1983. *Adabiyat-e Namayeshi dar Iran* [Dramatic Literature in Iran]. Vol. 2. Tehran: Entesharat-e Tus.

Miner, Earl. 1972. "The Wild Man Through the Looking Glass." In *The Wild Man Within: An Image in Western Thought from Renaissance to Romanticism*, edited by Edward Dudley and Maximillian Novak. Pittsburgh: University of Pittsburgh Press.

Montesquieu. 1972 [1721-1758] *The Persian Letters*. Tr. and ed., J. Robert Loy. New York: World Publishing.

Mottahedeh, Roy. 1985. *The Mantle of the Prophet*. New York: Pantheon Books.

Naficy, Hamid. 1989. "Popular Culture in Exile: Iranians in Los Angeles." M.S.

_____. 1988. "Liminality, Exile, and Television: Iranian TV in the U.S." M.S.

_____. 1986. "Film Culture in the Islamic Republic of Iran." M.S.

_____. 1990. "Exile Discourse and Television: A Study of Syncretic Cultures: Iranian Television in Los Angeles." Ph.D. Dissertation, University of California, Los Angeles.

Newmann, Karen. 1987. "'And Wash That Ethiop White': Femininity and the Monstrous in Othello." In *Shakespeare Reproduced: The Text in History and Ideology*, edited by Jean Howard and Marion O'Conner. New York: Methuen.

Ngugi Wa Thiong'o. 1968. *A Grain of Wheat*. London: Hyneman.

Nixon, Rob. 1987. "Caribbean and African Appropriations of The Tempest." *Critical Inquiry*. Vol 13, pp. 557-578.

Rafasanjani, Hashemi (Hojjat-ol-Eslam). 1986-1987. "Honar-e Ta'atr dar Rasta-ye Bidari-ye Mellat-ha-ye Mahrum-e Jahan." [The Art of Theatre on the Side/Service of the Deprived People of the World]. *Faslnameh-ye Honar*, pp. 520-521.

Sa`edi, Gholamhoseyn. 1985. Otello dar Sarzamin-e Ajayeb [Othello in the Land of Wonders]. In Pardeh-daran-e Ai'ineh-afruz and Otello dar Sarzamin-e Ajayeb, Do Namyesh-nameh as Gholamhoseyn-e Sa`edi. Paris: Ketab-e Alefba.

_____. 1983a. "Ru-dar-ru'i ba Khodkoshi-ye Farhangi." [Confronting Cultural Suicide]. *Alefba* 3, pp. 1-7.

_____. 1984. "Namayesh dar Hokumat-e Namayeshi" [Theatre in a Theatrical State. *Alefba* 5, pp. 1-9.

_____. 1986 [1984]. "Interview." By Zia' Sedghi, for the Harvard University Oral History of Iran, conducted in Paris and London. In *Alefba* 7, pp. 70-139.

_____. 1983. "Degardissi va Raha'i-ye Avareh-ha" [Metamorphosis and Deliverance of the Exiled/Homeless]. *Alefba* 2, pp. 1-5.

_____. 1987 [1979]. "Honar-zada'i: Mohlek-tarin Zarbat bar Peykar-e Farhang-e Farda" [Artistic Liquidation: Deadliest Strike Against the Culture of Tomorrow]. *Daftarha-ye Azadi* 2 (1987): 17-21.

_____. 1987a [1979]. "Opozision Doshman Nist" [The Opposition Is Not The Enemy]. *Daftarha-ye Azadi* 2 (1987): 32-35.

Schwartz, Theodore. 1975. "Cultural Totemism: Ethnic Identity Primitive and Modern." In *Ethnic Identity Cultural Continuities and Change,* edited by George de Vos and Lola Romanucci-Ross. Palo Alto: Mayfield Publishing Company.

Shakespeare, William. 1984. *The Complete Plays of William Shakespeare.* New York: Chatham River Press,

Silverman, Kaja. 1983. *The Subject of Semiotics.* New York: Oxford University Press.

Southgate, Minoo. 1984. "Sa`edi: A Bibliography." In *Fear and Trembling,* by Gholamhoseyn Sa`edi, translated by Minoo Southgate. Washington: Three Continents Press.

_____. 1984. "The Negative Images of Blacks in Some Medieval Iranian Writings." *Iranian Studies* 17, pp. 3-36.

Sprengnether, Madelon. 1989. "The Boy Actor and Femininity in Anthony and Cleopatra." In *Shakespeare's Personality,* edited by Norman Holland, et. al. Berkeley: University of California Press.

Taylor, Gary, 1989. *Reinventing Shakespeare: A Cultural History, From the Restoration to the Present.* New York: Weidenfeld and Nicolson.

White, Hayden. "The Forms of Wildness: Archeology of an Idea." In *The Wild Man Within: An Image in Western Thought from Renaissance to Romanticism,* edited by Edward Dudley and Maximillian Novak. Pittsburgh: University of Pittsburgh Press.

Wiley, Elizabeth. 1989. "The Status of Women in Othello." In *Shakespeare: Text, Subtext, and Context*, edited by Ronald Dotterer.

GLOSSARY

Always present on the scene: Since the Islamic Revolution, this is an attribute in reference to the Iranian people by government officials for their participation in various political and social activities.

Amir Arsalan: Known as Amir Arsalan Namdar [famous]; a popular nineteenth-century romance.

Bejeweled rice: A colorful dish traditionally prepared for special occasions containing a variety of nuts and berries.

Cafe Deram, Cafe Kowkab, Aqa Reza Soheyla: Popular taverns for lower classes in Tehran.

Committee [Komiteh]: Islamic Revolution Committees were set up throughout the country and exercised a wide range of authority to implement the new laws and regulations of the Islamic Revolution.

Congratulations and condolences: Offered simultaneously on the death of "martyrs" of the revolution.

Fajr, Fath...Operation: Actual names of Iranian military operations during the war against Iraq.

Haji: An honorific given to males who have made a pilgrimage to Mecca.

Hezbollahi sister: Reference to women who serve in official or semi-official capacities for the Revolutionary Committees or those committed to the cause of the Islamic Revolution.

Hidden Imam: See *Imam of the Age*.

Hypocrite: Derogatory reference to a member of the People's Mojahedin Organization, who oppose the rulers of the Islamic regime.

Imam of the Age: Refers to the Shi'ite twelfth imam, who is believed to have been in occultation since 837 AD. Shi'ites believe that he occasionally appears in order to help believers. In this play, Sa'edi depicts a reported ploy of the Islamic government of Iran to employ actors to play the Imam of the Age in order to boost the morale of Iranian fighters in the war.

Infirm Holy Imam: Reference to the fourth Shi'ite imam, son of Imam Hoseyn, the only male member of Hoseyn's family who was not killed in the battle in Karbala against the army of the Omayyad Calif, Yazid; he is referred to as "infirm" due to illness.

Jabalqa: A mythical city in the East beyond which no inhabitants exist.

Jabalsa: A mythical city in the West beyond which no inhabitants exist.

Karbala: A city in Iraq and the site for the shrine of Imam Hoseyn, the third Shi'ite imam, whose martyrdom is commemorated by Shi'ites every year.

Kowsar Pond: A pond in Paradise at which it is believe that Ali, the first Shi'ite imam and the son-in-law of the prophet, Mohammad, will stand and distribute water to the faithful.

Leader of the Oppressed of the World: Reference to Ayatollah Ruhollah Khomeyni, the leader of the Islamic Revolution in Iran in 1978-79.

Nest of Spies: Name given to the American Embassy in Tehran after it was taken over by revolutionaries.

Omm-e Leyla: Arabic phrase, literally "Mother of Leyla"; used by the MINISTER in place of the name Ophelia, because it is more familiar.

Rostam: The best-known legendary hero of the Persian epic, *Shahnameh* [Book of Kings], by the famous eleventh-century Iranian poet Ferdowsi.

Sam, son of Nariman: A hero in the *Book of Kings*.

Samsamossaltaneh, Saltanatossadat, Haj Aqa Kamal Qomeshchi: Names indicating to Persian speakers prominent people in the community.

Sherbet of martyrdom: The Persian expression "sharbat-e shahadat nushidan" literally means "drinking the sherbet of martyrdom", i.e., becoming a martyr. In this case, the metaphoric meaning of the expression is accompanied by a literal interpretation as well.

Shiruyeh: Son of Khosrow Parviz, the Sassanian (226-641 A.D.) king.

Sohrab: Refers to the story of Rostam and Sohrab in their battle immortalized in Ferdowsi's *Book of Kings*. Sohrab was the son of Rostam, who was killed by him not knowing that Sohrab was his son.

Tyrant: Reference to the deposed shah, Mohammad Reza Pahlavi.

Voice and Vision of the Islamic Republic: Official Iranian radio and television networks.

War of Truth Against Falsehood: Reference to the Iran-Iraq war, but sometimes the battle of the Islamic Republic against its enemies in general.

Yazid: The Omayyad calif whose army defeated Imam Hoseyn and his supporters in Karbala, Iraq, in 680 AD.

Zeynab sister: Zeynab was the heroic sister of Imam Hoseyn; a Zeynab sister, therefore, is any female who actively participates in implementing the Islamic laws and regulations.